JOHN ADAMS' PROMISE

How to Have Good Schools for <u>All</u> Our Children, Not Just for Some

Jon Saphier

TEACHERS[21]

Research for Better Teaching, Inc.

John Adams' Promise:
How to Have Good Schools for All Our Children, Not Just for Some

ISBN 1-886822-08-5

Distributed by:

Research for Better Teaching, Inc.
One Acton Place
Acton, Massachusetts 01720
978-263-9449 voice
978-263-9959 fax
info@rbteach.com e-mail

This publication is a collaborative project of Research for Better Teaching (www.rbteach.com) and Teachers[21] (www.Teachers21.org).

Research for Better Teaching (RBT) is an educational training and consulting firm dedicated to the professionalization of teaching. RBT consultants work with schools and school districts to improve the quality of teaching and leadership and to incorporate the study of teaching as an ongoing part of the district culture.

Teachers[21] is a national, non-profit educational consulting organization taking leadership in strengthening teacher quality. Teachers[21] is dedicated to systemic school improvement that is aligned with a well-researched knowledge base on teaching and a knowledge base on leadership.

Executive Summary

Evidence for the following propositions are presented in this essay:

1. We have legions of dedicated people in teaching, but we have a broken system for building their capacity and offering them opportunities to grow in high functioning workplaces. Therefore, not enough of our teachers have the requisite expertise to reach all our children.

2. The most significant influence on student achievement is the expertise of the individual teacher — what the person knows, believes and can do. And teaching expertise is far more complex, extensive, and sophisticated than we have acknowledged and put into actual classroom practice.

3. Teaching expertise includes *anything* a teacher does to increase the probability of intended learning. That is a great deal more than knowing your content, presenting it, and testing students. There is a common core of essential professional knowledge, immense but practical and accessible, that comprises "expertise in teaching." (see pp. 15-17 and Appendix A.) It is real; it is validated; it is field-tested. The accountability and the capacity to develop this expertise, however, are missing in action from most teacher education, teacher licensure, teacher evaluation, and professional development; yet it is the most highly leveraged commitment we could make for improving student achievement.

4. Our least prepared and least supported teachers work with our most needy students. Thus schools for the poor are a revolving door for teachers, half of whom leave within their first five years.

5. Our public schools are doing a decent job for the affluent but an inadequate job for the working class and children of poverty. This inequity is at great cost to our entire nation — economic as well as moral cost.

6. The reforms in the 1990s for higher standards and more accountability for public schools were needed. They were important initiatives, but our rural and urban poor students still graduate four grade levels behind their suburban peers. This is unacceptable. Standards and accountability are only half the job. Now we have to build the capacity to meet the standards for which we are holding people accountable.

7. Widely accepted is the myth that poor children are too far behind and too disadvantaged, or perhaps too intellectually weak to catch up, no matter what we do for their schools. In reality, we have proof that poor children are intellectually able to meet rigorous standards, even from severely disadvantaged

neighborhoods if: (a) their teachers have enough expertise; (b) staff take collective responsibility for student success; and (c) the school supports a motivational environment for students.

8. The individual school-as-workplace has a particularly high-leverage influence on teacher capacity if it operates as a professional culture of true collaboration. School-level leadership, especially by principals, is the fulcrum for building that workplace culture. Developing such leaders is too important to be a second tier priority.

After readers have considered the ideas in this monograph, I encourage them to:

- actively influence legislators, policy makers, and private funders to be guided by the central importance of knowledge-based teaching expertise and school based leadership in their decision-making.
- lobby legislators to require high standards and accountability by teacher training institutions for their graduates' professional expertise as measured by performance; to craft legislation that makes teacher evaluation and professional development knowledge-based; and to give State Departments of Education the resources to provide high quality technical assistance to schools.
- elect school boards that will budget for comprehensive induction programs that keep new teachers and develop superior ones; hire superintendents who are committed to developing teaching expertise.
- urge foundations and other funders to support school districts that have comprehensive, integrated plans to increase skillful leadership by principals and others who can build strong organizational cultures (see Big Rock #2).
- persuade legislators and funders to provide incentives and grant programs to low performing schools that build student cultures of aspiration, confidence, pride, and responsibility in the context of longer school days and years.
- provide incentives and grant programs to districts that build career ladders for teachers and positions within schools that recognize a teacher's professional expertise and effectiveness with student learning.

For these recommendations to become reality, the American federal political structure requires that we:

- work state-by-state
- generate, in each state, a coalition of legislators, policy makers, educators, business leaders, public advocacy groups and media allies.

Table of Contents

Promises of Democracy

"Schools should teach a common body of knowledge that would give each student an equal chance in life. It is a free school system, it knows no distinction of rich and poor…it throws open its doors and spreads the table of its bounty for all children of the state…Education beyond all other devices of human origin, is the equalizer of the conditions of men, the great balance wheel of the social machinery."

– Horace Mann

"Horace Mann is rightly the patron saint of public education, not because of what he always managed to accomplish in Massachusetts but because of what he said in his reports [from visits to over 1000 schools.] He talked about the public schools having a leveling effect, that merit should be able to rise. There is, I think, a deep connection between Mann's vision and Jefferson's because both of them disliked the idea that the family into which you were born determined how you ended up in American life."

– E.D. Hirsh

John Adams' promise asserted that it would be the responsibility of government to ensure that opportunities for good education be available throughout the country to all citizens…and that the preservation of democracy depended on it. He enshrined this right to a good education for all children into the Massachusetts Constitution.

"The free common school system is the most American thing about America."

– Adlai Stevenson

"Wisdom and knowledge, as well as virtue, diffused generally among the body of the people being necessary for the preservation of their rights and liberties; and as these depend on spreading the opportunities and advantages of education in various parts of the country, and among the different orders of the people, it shall be the duty of legislators and magistrates in all future periods…not only to provide education, but to cherish its interests."

– Constitution of the Commonwealth of Massachusetts
written by John Adams

A Parable of Teaching Expertise

Runyon Arts High School is a small inner city high school with 300 students who are all known personally by their teachers. The counseling staff is strong. The school has an alliance with the business community that funds field trips to cultural sites around the city. Every student takes art every day in line with the arts theme of the school. The school has extra computers, and the building is clean and safe. Students like coming to school, and the drop out rate is lower than other city high schools. The teachers are caring individuals, but their teaching is poor to mediocre with the notable exception of two star faculty members in the social studies department. The academic achievement of the students is low and seems stuck in the marginal zone of "needs improvement" with a very few students climbing to "proficient."

Across town is Daimler High School, a comprehensive 9-12 school of moderate size (800 students) and few resources. Its science laboratory is antiquated so that some experiments in the hand-on physics and chemistry courses are difficult to conduct. However, the teaching staff consists of a large number of men and women with highly developed teaching expertise, both generic teaching skills and skills specific to teaching their content areas. They not only teach their content well but also teach students to believe in themselves and to exert effective effort. They have created a culture among students of respect, pride, aspiration, and achievement. The student body at Daimler, although similar to Runyon in demographics, outperforms the kids at the Runyon by a considerable margin, both in test scores and number of kids who go on to post secondary education. Daimler's meager school budget does include funds for professional development and the salaries of two full-time instructional specialists. These specialists spend 80% of their time with teachers in classroom visits for observing, co-teaching, and presenting demonstration lessons. They work with teams analyzing student work and developing new teaching approaches, as well as facilitating planning among groups of teachers for group observations and debriefings. The principal has worked diligently to build a culture of honesty and non-defensiveness among faculty and to build powerful connections to parents.

The teachers manifest persistence to a high degree. The teachers "live" these qualities in their team meetings. This can be observed in their focus on how the students are doing and how they, the teachers, can improve their instruction. The assets at Runyon Arts are wonderful and good for students. Any school that has assembled these assets should be proud, but they are not enough. In fact, they are not even central to student achievement. Daimler has fewer resources, but it has the most important one—*teaching expertise*—which includes the capacity to build a strong student culture of achievement for students from disadvantaged backgrounds. It also has the organizational culture to continuously strengthen and improve this expertise. These are the things that matter most for student learning and achievement.

Introduction

The audiences for this monograph are leaders in school districts, school board members, college deans, as well as state and federal policy makers. It is offered to anyone who is interested in the professionalization of teaching to improve student results. The purpose of this monograph is to persuade readers to move the "Big Rocks" issues, to be described below, to the front of their agendas for education reform. We *needed* standards and we *needed* accountability. But we have left off the third leg[1] of the Education Reform movement: teaching expertise that is far more complex and sophisticated than acknowledged and that continues to be very unevenly distributed. The personnel systems that builds our teacher and administrator workforce are dysfunctional. These systems include teacher preparation, licensing, induction, evaluation, and professional development; they are not connected to one another, nor to the knowledge base of professional practice. These systems must be addressed as part of a comprehensive, long-term effort to improve educational outcomes for children.

The "teacher quality" movement is long overdue and is well-aimed at what should be the focus for improving schools; but the vocabulary lays traps. The phrase "quality teachers" allows many to focus on getting "better quality people," as if just having smarter people with more content education would fix our low performing schools. The qualification that matters for a "highly qualified teacher" is *expertise*—what they know, believe, and can do—not their pedigree or the letters after their name.

There's nothing wrong with the "quality" of most of the people we have. There's plenty wrong with the system that prepares our teachers for their role and ensures their constant increase in capacity. Getting "better people" cast into these same roles with similar deficits in knowledge-based expertise will have the same short-falls in student results we get now. So let's be careful of our vocabulary and focus on what matters most—what individual teaches know, believe, and can do—*teaching expertise*—and all the levers of influence on increasing that (see Essay Two).

[1] The three legged stool is an old New England metaphor. No matter how sturdy the first two legs, without the third leg, the stool cannot stand.

Some things matter more than others. If we wish to improve schools for all the children, we have to prioritize where we focus our time and energy because there is just so much of it to go around. The priorities for action are to:

I. Recognize the common core of professional knowledge about teaching and learning that comprises "expertise in teaching." Seize it and use it. Make it readily accessible to educators everywhere. Organize everything we do around the improvement of teachers' expertise at using it and contributing to it. Therefore, yoke together the ten systems that influence teacher quality[2] and ground them all in professional knowledge.

II. Explicitly teach school leaders the skills for building human working environments for adults that are collaborative, supportive, and results-oriented. That means focusing on the relationships and practices that make commitment to students and the improvement of teaching and learning through teamwork the absolute center of school operations. Evaluate these leaders on how well they do at creating such a professional culture.

III. Raise salaries by half for staff serving disadvantaged children, and by half again for those who are most effective (Miller 2004). Differentiate leadership roles for teachers so that responsibility and salary recognize expertise and so that professionals have a career ladder that promises them advancement without leaving teaching. (Milken 1999; Wise 2004.)

These three "Big Rocks" for school improvement need to go together. They enable one another, and together they are the package that will dramatically elevate student achievement.

The first essay of this monograph profiles the knowledge it takes to actualize these three recommendations

The second essay describes the processes necessary to bring the knowledge to life.

The third essay reports a seven-year case study of a 192 school multiethnic district that has made substantial progress on the agenda of this book.

[2] The ten systems are: 1) Teacher Education (Graduate and Undergraduate), 2) Licensing and Certification, 3) Recruiting and Hiring, 4) Induction, 5) Continuing Education and Professional Development, 6) Teacher Evaluation, 7) Recertification, 8) Teacher Advancement, 9) Structuring of the School, and 10) Culture of the School and Professional Community.

What Jim Rodriguez, the new Superintendent of Schools, said to all his administrators at the Summer Retreat

"Teaching expertise is what matters most; and we know what it consists of—what it looks and sounds like. It's got a common core of elements, and our teachers need them all:

- expertise at motivation;
- expertise at using cognitive science;
- expertise at class management;
- expertise at instructional design;
- expertise at content specific pedagogy; and
- expertise at analysis of concepts in lessons from students' point of view."

"I don't care how you get your people to possess this expertise. Hire it; send people out to get it; develop it internally with good PD [professional development]; build an infrastructure of experts who coach everybody on it . . . any or all of the above or another way you invent. Just get it and get it used by the people who are with the children every day."

ESSAY 1

The Three Big Rocks of Education Reform

The Need for Good Teaching for America's Poorest Children: Where Social Justice and Economic Self-Interest Come Together

A futurist of my acquaintance once started a workshop by filling a giant glass jar with rocks. The jar was about two feet high and very wide, and the rocks were between the size of golf balls and baseballs. When the level of the rocks reached the lip of the jar, the presenter asked us if we thought the jar was now full. We said, "Yes".

Then he pulled out a tray of gravel from under the table and proceeded to pour in a cupful, shake the gravel down between the cracks in the rocks, and then put in many more cupfuls. He then looked at us and asked if we thought the jar was full. We nodded a hesitant "yes".

Then he pulled out a tray of sand and proceeded to ladle in many cupfuls, pausing to shake the sand in between the cracks until the jar was...full? "Probably not," we said.

And, indeed, he then pulled out a tray of water and poured in over a quart before the water leveled off at the top.

I never forgot the point of his story. It went something like this: "If I hadn't put in the big rocks first, I never would have had room for all the other stuff. But when I started with the big rocks, there was plenty of room later for the other smaller items to sift down in between them."

Ever since that day, I have thought of this analogy of the "big rocks" when trying to sift through educational innovations. What are the "big rocks" of school improvement? What things are more important than others and will allow room for all the other good things to sift into place?

What I see now is that, while my colleagues and I have worked on many good things over the last three decades, we have not yet "filled the jar". The standards movement alone, as much as it was needed, has not budged student performance much in big city schools or narrowed the achievement gap for children of poverty and children of color. It is time to put our efforts in perspective and focus on the missing "big rocks".

Dramatically improving low performing schools, especially for children of poverty, is a demanding but doable task and essential to preserving our national unity, our economic vitality, and our democracy. It is the most important domestic priority of the next 20 years. This is said with mindfulness and respect of the great need for national health care and a secure retirement system[3].

The promise of American democracy has always been a fair chance at a good life if you work hard and take advantage of the opportunities of a free society. This is no longer true in our country. Children of poverty, especially in our cities, do not get their fair chance because they do not get the education that would give it to them. For working class children, the problem is just as serious but less visible. Many receive mediocre educations that leave undeveloped the vision and promise our schools could deliver.

Ten million children in urban and poor schools in this country are four grade levels or more behind in basic literacy and math skills (Haycock, 2004; Thernstrom and Thernstrom 2003). That is one fifth of all the children. But John Adams' promise for a good education was not just (or even particularly) for the poor. Working class children live in families where disposable income has declined steadily for twenty years despite the overall increase in national wealth and the shift to dual wage-earner families. (Jencks 2004; Phillips 2002). These families see the possibilities for social mobility, that were so important to their parents, disappearing for their children. They do not see clearly that their children are not pressed hard or taught well enough to achieve the levels of excellence that would enable the "better life" that American education was always supposed to offer.

I grew up in the shadow of the depression with working class grandparents who taught me from deep belief that doing well in school was my job and my ticket to an unlimited future. As first generation Irish Catholic and Dutch Jewish immigrants, they taught me more than my parents did about the land of opportunity. They went to public schools in New York City where most of them, including my

[3] George Kennan was a wise, philosophical, experienced State Department hand. In the course of an interview somebody asked him what our foreign policy should be during the Clinton administration. He thought for a minute and said that the best foreign policy the United states can have is to get its own house in order. (Max DePree, Leading Without Power.)

mother, could not afford to finish high school. America *did* become a land of opportunity for them, and ultimately, for me. My forebears were white so it was easier for them than for people of color. But historically, the value of an education has been even stronger in the African-American community as it rose out of slavery (Perry et al. 2003); and it has continued to be so until quite recent times. Living out of this consciousness is probably more alive in Black America than anywhere in our society. Nor is this consciousness missing in Hispanic America. In San Diego, for example, legions of Mexican families cross the border weekly to work as domestics and laborers so their children can get an education in American schools.

Here is my point: the promise of making the life you can dream for yourself and for your children has its roots in good education. Our current system does not have the capacity to deliver on that promise. And it doesn't have to be that way.

This situation is not new, and dealing with it has stymied reformers for half a century, despite the United States being the wealthiest country in the world. Twenty-five years ago, Ron Edmonds (1978) said we already had the knowledge to remedy the achievement gap of our poorest children, but lacked the political will. He may have been right about the political will; I am not sure that he was right then about the knowledge. But we *do* have the knowledge now. Some have believed the problem to be intractable because of the magnitude of social problems bred by poverty (Traub 2000.) We also know now that this is not true. Against the worst odds and in the most devastated neighborhoods, we can find schools where poor children's learning is accelerated past their initial disadvantages (Charles A. Dana Center 1999; NASSP 2004; Minkoff 2003; Jerald 2001). The children in these schools equal or outperform their more affluent suburban peers. These schools, however, are like bright burning candles: they get great results and usually flame out within 10 years or less. Their examples are never brought to scale in their cities or districts.

Our urban and our poor schools "underperform" not just because the children come from deprived backgrounds, but because we fail to provide their teachers with enough teaching expertise to do what needs to be done. This is not meant to diminish the daunting obstacles to academic achievement that face children in severely disadvantaged neighborhoods. I acknowledge the need, so well articulated by Richard Rothstein (2004), for national policies that address the social, economic, health and nutrition issues of children of poverty. School improvement alone is not enough to solve the problems of poverty in

12% of our school age population, now, is Hispanic. In 2025, it will be 25%. In that same year, 53% of our total school age population will be children of color. Does anyone really think that white males – by then 20% of the workforce – will be able to carry this nation economically? Do we really think we can afford not to have an educated workforce across the board? We could get by without it as recently as the 70s, but no more.

The global marketplace and our own new demographics have changed everything. Thanks to technology, we can now move the work to where the workers are – not just information and service work either. Only 30% of India's population gets a good education, but that's 300 million people – more than the entire population of the United States!

To remain competitive, we have to graduate H.S. seniors who are prepared for the modern workplace. So how are our schools doing? Not so well.

Right now we have an achievement gap of four grade levels between affluent communities and poor communities, between white suburbs and communities with children of color.

America. But school improvement could easily become a doorway out of poverty for a generation of children who deserve a chance and aren't getting it. We should at least get this part of our national agenda right and do it now. We have the knowledge, we have the talent, and we have the resources.

Large numbers of poor children throughout our urban and rural systems are far behind academically, but they are not condemned to stay there. That is the message of the high performing urban schools cited previously, schools that have proven that children's learning can be accelerated to make up the deficits with which their environments have saddled them. To act otherwise is to deny the data and to create a dead-end, which Walter Lippmann described long ago in the pages of the New Republic (1928), in which he warned we could create "generations of students and educators who don't believe that those who begin weak can ever become strong." We are in danger of fulfilling this prophecy.

It is false to say our schools are failing across the board. We rank second in the world for 4th grade literacy, fourth for 8th grade achievement, and in the middle for high school results (Sherman, et al. 2003) when compared to the most advanced industrial democracies in the world. Our suburban schools are doing all right, at least in literacy. But our city schools *are* failing the children, and it is not their fault! As a society, we have not honored the commitment of our forebears to equal opportunity. Thus, we have not mustered the political will and economic resources to build the personnel systems that could make all our schools work.

Let me put this in perspective. We have made certain choices in our history about what role our government should play in guaranteeing rights to all its citizens. For example, workers have a right to a base-line retirement income through social security. Yet our children do not have a right to a minimum standard of living; they do not have a right to guaranteed health care; they don't even have a right to clean water! But they *do* have a right to a good education. That was the promise of John Adams and a commitment represented today in the rhetoric of "No Child Left Behind". We have the knowledge and the resources to deliver on this promise; but we do not. We must change that if we are to remain a strong country and a real democracy. This is both a moral and an economic imperative. What is our government *for* if not to assure equality of opportunity in this rich nation of resources and promise? That is the American dream—true equal opportunity if you work hard to make something of yourself.

> "The leading object of government is to lift artificial weights from all shoulders...to afford all an unfettered start and a fair chance in the race of life."
>
> – Abraham Lincoln[4]

How we treat our poorest and most oppressed people is the measure of our society and its moral fibre. This was the message of the prophet Amos, of Jesus, of Martin Luther King, Jr., of Abraham Lincoln, and of modern writers like Robert Bellah.

The economic argument lines up in parallel, not opposition, to the moral one. We see the needs of the workplace behind the drive and large commitment that American industry has made to improving our education system. Corporate giants like Boeing, Motorola, IBM and dozens of others make significant contributions annually to improving public education. Business leaders know that in the information economy of the 21st century they can no longer hire the workers that they need when the majority of our high school graduates are below proficiency in literacy (Daggett 2002). They spend $80 billion annually providing these skills to entry-level employees. It did not matter as much in an industrial economy where factory workers did not need high literacy skills, but it does now (Daggett 2002; Murnane and Levy 1995; Hershberg 1997).

Put simply, in addition to the moral and civic obligation to make good on the promise of our democracy, it is in the direct economic interest of the affluent suburban electorate and of corporate America that poor city kids get a good education. Instead, city children now get the least prepared teachers who teach in poor working conditions with fewer resources than their colleagues in more affluent districts. (Darling-Hammond 1996)

To succeed in improving schools for children of poverty, we need to get our priorities right. There are so many dimensions to the problem that it is easy to get distracted by important but not

The gap is widening, not narrowing. 17 year old Hispanic and African -Americans' scores are comparable to white 13 year olds' on NAEP math, the most reliable nation-wide measure we have of student achievement over time. And these students represent the majority of the workforce that is going to pay all our social security.

These statistics don't just spotlight public schools. 47% of this years college freshmen will take 1 or more remedial courses. Only 55% of kids who enter 2-year colleges will be back for the second year. That's a 45% drop out rate. How about AYP (adequate yearly progress scores) for higher education?
26% of kids who enter 4-year colleges drop out after the first year; and 60% overall drop out before graduation.
And of those who *do* graduate:
43% of science degrees are awarded to non-U.S. citizens.
42% of mathematics degrees are awarded to non-U.S. citizens.
46% of computer science degrees are awarded to non-U.S. citizens.
36% of physics degrees are awarded to non-U.S. citizens.
56% of engineering degrees are awarded to non-U.S. citizens.
And remember the 40+% college graduation rate we *do* have includes all those non-US citizens!

—Willard Daggett.
Presented at the 2004 Model Schools Conference, © International Center for Leadership in Education.

[4] Special session message, July 4, 1861.

"Human capital, as Lester Thurow, Robert Reich, and many others have argued, will be the source of comparative advantage in the 21st century global economy. Although the overall U.S. economy has done well over the past 25 years, not all Americans shared equally in its rewards. The top fifth of American families were the overwhelming beneficiaries—the bottom three-fifths lost ground and the second fifth were largely stagnant—and the resulting income inequality threatens the long-term viability of our economy and the stability of our democracy.

Economists are generally agreed that although the sources of this inequality are many—an eroding minimum wage, the declining power of unions to win large settlements at the bargaining table, and growing global competition—fully half the explanation can be attributed to "new technologies that favor the better educated."

Our schools always did one thing well: They educated the top fifth of their students. The performance of the remaining 80 percent didn't matter because, upon leaving school, they entered a robust manufacturing economy that provided abundant jobs for those with limited skills. Although the work was hard, the pay was good—good enough after World War II and into the 1960s for the wife of a typical blue-collar worker to stay at home and raise the kids and still have enough left over for the family to buy a boat or recreational vehicle.

But those days are gone, and they are not coming back. According to the 1990 book *America's Choice: High Skills or Low Wages*, if companies around the globe can now buy foolproof machinery to compensate for deficient worker skills, and if people in other countries using this machinery will work for $5 a day, let alone the $10 or $15 an hour that American workers want, we cannot compete on the basis of wage. We can only compete on the basis of skill.

The end of the manufacturing era, with its well-paying jobs for people with limited skills, means that our schools must now educate *all* our children to a level never required before. For over a century, our schools taught millions upon millions of immigrants and farmers to respect authority, to show up on time, to work hard, and to repeat monotonous tasks. In short, schools were the vehicle through which an entire labor force was socialized to accept the discipline of the industrial era.

But these are not the skills needed in a postindustrial, global economy. The battleground of the future will be economic, not military. Nations are fighting for domination of the high-value-added industries—computers and software, robotics, civilian aviation, synthetic materials, microelectronics, biotechnology, and telecommunications—that pay high wages and offer their employees living standards American workers have grown to expect.

While we still desire a strong work ethic, we must appreciate the implications for education of an economy that changes with striking and unprecedented rapidity. This rapidly changing economy requires workers who are flexible, adaptable, quick learners, critical thinkers and above all else, problem-solvers. *And these are precisely the skills our schools are not teaching.*

Most suburban residents compare their schools with those of the big cities they surround. Because on average they have lower dropout rates, better achievement scores and higher college-enrollment rates, suburbanites conclude their schools are fine and the problems reside in the cities. Unfortunately, there is no comfort in this suburban-to-urban comparison. Worse, this comparison functions as a sedative, a soporific that has put Americans to sleep. It has left us complacent, thinking that the education problem lies elsewhere, in our cities with their large, poor, disproportionately nonwhite populations.

Ample evidence from the National Academy of Sciences' Third International Mathematics and Science Study and the results from the internationally benchmarked reference exams developed by the national New Standards project make clear that nowhere in America—even in our best school districts—are the majority of students performing at world-class levels.

The floor on which Americans have been standing for the past two decades has been tilting, and people without real skills have been sliding to reduced-wage levels. The angle of the tilt in this floor will grow sharper with each passing year as global trade and technology advance. If we want to anchor our children to firm economic ground, we'll have to provide them with lifelines fashioned of genuine skill and high-quality education."

– Theodore Hershberg, *Education Week*, December 10, 1997. Reprinted with permission.

central issues. We have not, I believe, focused on the central issues up to this point. That is the reason for this monograph.

To get the achievement results we want for children in urban and poor communities, the overriding goal and one guiding principle that we need to keep in view as we work on any question, consider any program, change any structure is that: *everything hinges on improving the teaching expertise of the individual teachers who work with the children.* We must recognize that teaching expertise is far more complicated and sophisticated than we have acknowledged.

Teaching is intellectually complicated, difficult and demanding work with as many elements in successful practice as one finds in engineering, law, architecture, or any knowledge-based profession. Later in this monograph, I will attempt, with some trepidation, to describe the scope of this knowledge base in six pages (See Appendix A)[5]. The range of variables for which teachers need well-developed skills is far wider than our voting public understands when it debates school budgets.

To make an analogy, imagine an automobile where we want to improve poor or mediocre gas mileage (replace with student achievement). What factors bear on mileage? The following do, simultaneously and interactively: proper spark plug gap; dirty or clean carburetor jets; correct octane of fuel; wear on manifold gasket; correctness of tire pressure; driving habits (jerky or smooth); cylinder pressure (are the cylinder rings still tight?); leaks in gas lines; cleanliness of fuel filter; ignition timing; (I could go on…). Every one of these is PROVEN CLINICALLY to improve gas mileage if optimized (same for each of the tasks of teaching described in the sections to follow). But peak gas mileage is only attained if ALL of them are in good shape. And if gas mileage is very poor, improving a few of them will make a dent but perhaps only a small dent in the problem. And some factors are probably more important than others (e.g., fixing the gas leak.) Fixing any constellation of these variables, if one hits enough of them, will improve performance. Exactly the same can be said for the fifty-plus tasks of teaching and all the knowledge and skills in generic and content-specific pedagogy that will be presented in this monograph.

Making teaching expertise the focus of national and state policy will

[5] Elsewhere (Saphier and Gower 1997) I have struggled to do so in 600 pages.

reframe and potentiate all the other important things we are doing around standards, leadership, resources, and teacher quality.

The task is complicated and multi-faceted enough so that we must focus on the "big rocks", the most essential levers on improvement. So what are they? Small schools? Lesson study? Block scheduling? Reading across the curriculum? School choice? Site-based decision-making? Parent-involvement programs? These and dozens of other programs are all important, all good, all worthwhile. But they are not the "big rocks". They are significant stones, good vehicles for school improvement if the "big rocks" are in place. None of them alone will make much difference. And each and every one of them will be multiplied in potency if the "big rocks" are in the jar.

I have selected three "big rocks" for highlighting because I believe focusing on them is the only way that we will create the space in the jar for all the other good programs ... and the only way our public schools can fulfill their promise, namely, a fair chance at a good life for all our children through equal educational opportunity. The three "big rocks" are: (1) teaching expertise based on professional knowledge, (2) leadership skills for strong organizational culture, and (3) higher salaries and differentiated career paths for teachers.

"Big Rock" #1: Expertise Based on Professional Knowledge

An accessible common core of professional knowledge exists for the development of expertise in teaching. Expertise in teaching—what individual teachers know, believe and can do—matters more than any variable in student achievement. It is not the only one, but it is the defining one. The data on teacher effects is clear and consistent (Gross 1999; Mendro 2000; Muijis and Reynolds 2000; Sanders and Rivers 1996). Too few of our teachers have enough expertise, and our poorest children have the largest share of low-expertise teachers. (Darling-Hammond 1996).

Sanders' research and follow-up studies by others at other sites showed startling findings: regardless of their starting academic level, students who have three high-gain teachers in a row wind up performing fifty percentile points higher than matched students who have three low-gain teachers in succession. This same "value-added" research, however, did not reveal what successful teachers do. The Sanders studies only identified that some teachers reliably outperform others in producing student learning, not *what* successful teachers do to get these results!

Designing observational studies to find the commonalities of what these people do, however, would probably only reproduce the tepid findings of the 1960s and 1970s when such research on teaching had its heyday (Dunkin and Biddle 1974). Because of the erroneous approach we took to determine "effective" teaching in the late 20'h century, we missed the fact that we were building a powerful knowledge base for practice despite failing to profile the "effective" teacher. I will expand on this point shortly.

My main point is that *there is already a common core of professional knowledge about teaching and learning that comprises "expertise in teaching."* It is different in character from simple lists of "effective behavior," and it is far more complex and sophisticated than we have allowed. There is not enough teaching expertise from this common core resident in enough teachers to educate all our children. It is not even readily accessible to most of them in poor and rural areas. This expertise gap is the root cause of the inequality that public education delivers to children across America; and let there be no doubt: it is, indeed, unequal (Carroll, et al. 2004). In making this case, I will not ignore the powerful forces of poverty that blight large parts of our nation. But I will make the case, already supported by data, that it does not make as much difference as some people want it to make; and that with appropriate focus of our resources, American public schools can be an opportunity machine far beyond what they are now.

So "big rock" #1 is to recognize this common core of professional knowledge, claim it, and organize everything we do around the improvement of teachers' expertise at acquiring it, using it and enlarging it. This common core can be built into teacher education, teacher licensure, and into district systems for new teacher induction, teacher evaluation, on-going professional development and career advancement. But it presently is not.

Demand to unify the common core of knowledge about medicine occurred as a result of the Flexner Report in 1910. The report caused a sea-change that revolutionized medical education and, consequently, the standards for admission into the profession (Starr 1982). Medical education became a knowledge- based system built on extensive clinical practice, close continual supervision, and gradual assumption of responsibility for client welfare. This was not a radical concept then, nor is it today. On the contrary, using professional knowledge to create standards of practice is quite a conventional idea. The result of agreeing on knowledge-based standards in medicine was a profession that today earns public trust and whose performance is the envy of the world. It is time to do the same for education.

Let me begin by outlining the scope of this common core of professional knowledge on teaching and learning before describing each domain in detail. The knowledge base for successful teaching is far bigger than any undergraduate program (or any 5th year program for that matter) could contain. We cannot expect teacher education to be completed by the undergraduate and graduate study that goes into the initial licensing process. We do not expect that for other professions where our society acknowledges the complexity of good practice. The same will become true for the path into teaching when we acknowledge the extensive nature of the professional knowledge that it takes to do the job well. Just as highly skilled practitioners do not emerge up and running from medical school, we cannot expect beginning teachers to graduate as high functioning professionals.

Many readers who have succeeded in life believe themselves to be well educated and may not think that their teachers did anything complex or extraordinary. "They had high expectations and just gave us the material clearly." This attitude leads to the prevailing idea that any decent, literate person can step into a classroom and learn the "tricks of the teaching trade" in a year or two. But tricks of the trade will not do for most students, at least not if we are serious about the standards movement and educating all our children to proficiency levels in major subject areas. Motivated children from literate homes may do all right with teachers who bring common sense but no professional expertise to the job. This is not so, however, for the majority of our children and especially for those students who are poor. Yet we entrust many beginning teachers, unprepared as they are, with the reading and writing instruction of children who will suffer devastating limits on their future lives if they do not acquire proficient literacy skills. We need to expect, and even demand, that their teacher preparation be based on a common core of essential professional knowledge. Only then can we effectively structure the entrance of novices into the profession along with their continuing growth and gradual assumption of responsibilities.

Now let me offer a definition of teaching: *Teaching expertise is anything a teacher does that influences the probability of intended student learning.*

This definition allows us to acknowledge the extraordinary array of skills successful teachers bring to their work, an array far beyond being a content expert who presents material and gives tests. It allows us to include a spectrum all the way from the skills for building a humane and caring environment to those of cognitive science that scaffold concepts and maximize student construction of meaning . . . from the skills of data analysis about student work to the skills for teaching students to believe in themselves and study effectively.

Expertise in a complex profession *does not* consist of executing "effective" behaviors. *Expertise consists in making choices and making decisions based on expert knowledge.* These choices are drawn from an extensive repertoire of approaches and practices: a repertoire that beginners do not have no matter how talented or dedicated they may be. They are choices that are a good match for the students, the curriculum, and/or the context. So teaching expertise is about making decisions and choices. Expert teachers are always seeking to broaden their repertoires for making these choices. They are also constantly finding new questions and new professional frontiers to explore. One area mastered then reveals the next one to learn and to integrate (Bereiter and Scardamalia 1993.)

Potent evidence of the importance of teacher expertise at making these choices comes from research on successful teachers of beginning reading (Pressley et al. 1998). The most effective reading teachers draw on methods from the different mainstream approaches to reading: phonemic awareness and phonics, linguistics, explicit comprehension skills instruction, whole language, and meaning emphasis. "These teachers were often quite explicit when developing word-level skills and strategies, but they also contextualized this explicit instruction in real reading and writing activities and tailored instruction to children's specific needs. Such instruction cannot be packaged in 'teacher-proof' curriculum materials." (Pressley 1998). The point is that teacher expertise makes the difference.

Six Areas of Teaching Expertise

Teaching expertise means having a repertoire of ways at one's disposal for handling the tasks of teaching, and then knowing how to choose and apply what is appropriate from one's repertoire. I have grouped the tasks into six categories: (1) Management, (2) Motivation, (3) Instruction, (4) Planning, (5) Applying Craft Knowledge for Teaching Specific Concepts and Skills, and (6) Understanding the Connections between Concepts in the Content and How Students Learn Them.

What follows is a description of each of the six global areas of teaching expertise. The elaborated list of tasks will come later, some 50 plus of them, for which we have convincing data. (See Appendix A for these tasks of teaching.) Each task separately is research validated, field tested, and known to impact student learning. Together they form the basis of our common core of professional knowledge. **N.B.: teaching skill does not mean executing specific behaviors; it means accomplishing 50+ tasks any way your repertoire equips you to do so.**

Management expertise means arranging the environment to maximize attention and engagement with the learning experiences. This is teacher as environmental engineer. Teachers need to know how to get students' attention and hold it, supported by planfully engineered rules, routines, procedures, and arrangements of time and space. If the classroom is not well managed, no one pays attention to the instruction no matter how good it is. There is no one right way to get students' attention and get rules and procedures in place, but there is

an extensive repertoire of strategies. Research confirms our common sense that, the more teachers explicitly handle these situations, the better is the student learning. But if management of classroom procedures is not practiced to some degree, learning does not take place at all.

Spiritual Leader & Psychologist

Motivational expertise pertains to teachers' ability to mobilize students' desire to learn, build their confidence and belief in themselves, and teach them how to exert effective effort. This is teacher as spiritual leader and psychologist. When students feel psychologically safe, able, and motivated to do well, they will do better work. The more teachers explicitly build these conditions into students' classroom lives, the more they learn. With firm management and wonderful instruction, learning still may not take place if the students do not want to learn, believe it is not worth their while, or spend all their energy consumed with feeling hostile, stupid or fearful of their peers.

Instructional expertise includes all the teacher dispositions and skills associated with getting inside the learners' heads; finding out what they know and do not know; surfacing their thinking; assessing and redesigning instruction based on how well the learners are learning. This is teacher as applied cognitive scientist and diagnostician. It includes skillful application of the hundreds of strategies derived from cognitive research such as modeling thinking aloud, periodic summarizing, application of classical learning principles, and frequent detailed feedback that students can use for improvement. It also includes a repertoire of powerful framing strategies to make new learning take and stick. Some are highly technical in nature and take extended practice and theoretical understanding to use well.

Planning expertise means applying highly developed skills of logic and design to daily lessons. This is teacher as architect of students' intellectual experience. Successful teachers plan backwards from the outcomes they want; thus, they create daily lessons that are tight designs of learning experiences precisely aligned with worthwhile, high-leverage objectives like knowing how to make and read a graph.[6] (Reeves 2002) and that are assessed frequently. The learning experiences are both engaging and effectively crafted vehicles of learning because they make the content accessible to the learners. Skillful planning originates in knowledge of one's curriculum and in one's knowledge of how to analyze class data on how the students as a group are doing, plus detailed knowledge of where one's students are as individuals in relation to intended learnings.

[6] A "high leverage objective" is one that has high use in life and transfer across disciplines. For example, one uses the ability to make and read graphs in the social sciences, in mathematics, and in all the physical sciences.

Craft knowledge for teaching specific concepts and skills was described two decades ago by Lee Shulman (1984) as Pedagogical Content Knowledge. This term described the knowledge that allows teachers to teach their particular content. This meant content-specific repertoires of activities, examples, stories, equipment, readings, analogies that make the concepts and skills accessible to students. Such knowledge is craft knowledge. It is accumulated slowly over years of experience, of experimentation, of trading ideas with colleagues, and from good professional development. Like the other domains of professional knowledge we have profiled above, pedagogical content knowledge consists of repertoires, not right or best ways.

Understanding the connections between the concepts and the content is another kind of knowledge related to the teaching of content that is different from the accumulated treasury of examples and instructional approaches we call pedagogical content knowledge. It is knowledge of how the concepts and skills one is teaching are connected to one another and how to bring these relationships to the attention of one's students. This includes an understanding of the network of concepts "that relate to the specific concept to be taught and of how that network is connected to the [content] in the yearlong curriculum as well as to the curricula of the previous and following years." (West and Staub 2003).

These six categories of teaching expertise that include the 50+ research validated tasks of teaching delineated in Appendix A can be said to form the Common Core of Professional Knowledge. As different as they are from one another, all six types are necessary. If any one of them is absent, learning will not take place for many students.

In addition to these six areas of teaching skill, there are other important knowledge bases that bear on teacher's success. Like the six areas above, these three are seldom found in teacher preparation programs or other systems that influence teacher capacity.

- Knowledge of individual differences in learners and how to include those differences in instructional decisions. These include cultural differences, developmental differences, and learning style differences.
- Knowledge of how to be a good colleague and team member.
- Knowledge of how to communicate effectively with parents and community.

Why Is This Core of Common Knowledge Not Acknowledged?

Great chunks of the common core of professional knowledge are missing in action from most teacher education, induction, and evaluation programs. How could this be so in an era of educational reform and supposedly strong commitment to improve American public education?

If you ask the wrong questions, you get the wrong answers. For the entire 20th century, we asked the wrong question, namely, what behaviors and practices make "effective" teaching? Commentators said again and again: There is no convincing or consistent research to back up any particular practices. We had no agreement among experts about what a common core of professional knowledge might be.

Have you noticed that no one asks: "What are the effective practices that make a good lawyer?" There is no demand to cite a research-backed list of "effective" practices and behaviors. There are no "effective practice" list for architects or engineers either. Why is that?

For one thing, we know practitioners in those fields have passed a rigorous examination administered by standards boards that are controlled by the profession itself. The profession acts as gate-keeper against shoddy practice. We trust these professions to certify people and protect the public against personnel who could damage clients. But we do not feel the need to have a "profession" of teaching because we do not believe it takes "professional knowledge" to do the job well; nor do we believe that well-meaning but unexpert practitioners could damage children. How wrong that is! At our children's peril we continue to believe that teaching is a low-level craft, easily learned and practiced well by smart college graduates who were highly successful students themselves. That is the problem because that belief is false, as so much evidence shows (Laczko-Kerr 2003).

The Nature of Professional Knowledge

Successful teaching and learning co-varies with the six areas of teaching expertise. What the research on teaching gives us is the inventory of tasks inside these areas that *do* make a difference in student learning. Each has a separate effect, and cumulatively and interactively, they account for how the learning is going. There exists a *repertoire* of moves or strategies from which individuals may draw to fulfill these tasks. The knowledge base on teaching and learning does not show, nor could it, that any *particular* strategy (say, using slates to check for understanding or teaching phonics to beginning readers) is inherently better (i.e., effective). But research tells us that applying *some* well-chosen strategies to handle the job (e.g., checking for understanding; developing letter sound correspondence) is essential.

Skillfulness in teaching derives from having large enough repertoires so that you are equipped to make choices in the major areas of performance that affect student learning. Once you have the repertoires, skillfulness means making choices thoughtfully based on reason, experience, and knowledge—making choices that are appropriate for a given student, situation, or curriculum. This is the nature of professional knowledge and its use in any profession. In a profession, you have to have knowledge of your clients, of your content, and of the array of tools particular to your craft in order to act with expertise and get good results for your clients. So it is with teaching.

Every one of the tasks of teaching identified in Appendix A bears positively and significantly on the achievement of the students in a classroom. They operate cumulatively and interactively. And there are a great many of them. Given the complexity of professional knowledge and what is expected from teachers in different contexts, it would be naïve to expect a study of successful teachers to come up with a simple or even a uniform profile of good teaching.

I believe that there are some teachers who are so good at motivating their students that they do startlingly well. Some teachers may have mediocre planning skills, may be undistinguished but adequate in instructional skills, but superb at inspiring confidence in their students. Still other teachers may be very highly developed at planning and instructional skills, so much so that most of their students do very well even though the teacher does not have a brilliant repertoire for the motivational tasks. Unfortunately, unnoticed by these teachers may be the discouraged or quietly unmotivated kids who slip through the cracks.

Since ALL the tasks of teaching bear on academic success of the students, many profiles of teachers with differential strengths in their expertise can combine to produce impressive student gains.

I previously cited the value-added methodology pioneered by William Sanders and colleagues that showed the most significant variable in student achievement was the classroom teacher. Students of equal-entering performance placed in the classes of high-performing teachers for three successive years score 50 percentile points above matched students placed in the classes of low-performing teachers. This is a huge difference that is enough to impact, significantly and permanently, the lives and future success of these children. These results have justifiably provoked renewed interest in teacher quality. If this interest spawns a new surge of observational research on teaching as was so active in the 1960s and 1970s, it will be important in the design of this research to recognize the complexity and multiplicity of the teaching variables operating on students.

Implications for Teacher Preparation and Professional Development

How does a person learn these six skill areas? Our pre-service teachers ought to be learning how to carry out some of these tasks in their undergraduate and graduate programs, but they must realistically continue their professional learning from colleagues and post-graduate professional development programs.

The first four domains of professional knowledge (Management, Motivation, Instruction, and Planning Expertise) described here are generic, (i.e., they are appropriate and applicable for all grade levels and in any subject). For these four domains we say that policy makers and teacher educators need: (1) to decide which parts of these four areas of the common core are best learned in pre-service teacher preparation, which during internship, and which in later career[7]; (2) to create institutes, academies, regional centers, on-line data bases so that access to this common core is available to all teachers all the time; and 3) to build connections of practitioners to one another through electronic libraries (Hiebert, Gallimore and Stigler[8]) so that

[7] It is my personal view that Planning Expertise is one area that could and should be mastered in the academic phase of preparation programs. My 30 years of classroom work on the ground with teachers, however, have shown it to be glaringly absent in huge numbers of beginning and veteran practitioners alike.

[8] "Collaboration, then, becomes essential for the development of professional knowledge, not because collaborations provide teachers with social support groups but because collaborations force their participants to make their knowledge public and understood by colleagues."

"To be successful...the research and development system (about teaching) needs to incorporate the expertise and unique skills of both teachers and researchers. Both communities would need to reorient their professional goals and values. Teachers would need to change their view that teaching is a personal and private activity and adopt the more risky but rewarding view that teaching is a professional activity that can be continuously improved if it is made public and examined openly.

James, Heibert, Ronald Gallimore, and James Stigler. *Educational Researcher*. A Knowledge Base for the Teaching Profession: What Would It Look Like and How Can We Get One? Vol. 31, Number 5, June/July 2002.

teachers in the field can continue to be constant contributors and refiners of the professional knowledge base.

For each academic subject at each level—early elementary, middle elementary, middle school, and high school—ask experts of pedagogical content knowledge to agree on what beginning teachers should know and be able to do, especially for literacy and mathematics instruction. This, of course, is no mean feat. It calls for unprecedented dialog, cooperation and consensus building between expert practitioners and the faculties of teacher preparation programs. That will never happen by itself. It will have to be induced by the pressure of public opinion, as happened in medicine, and by the incentives and pressure that can be brought by policy makers, legislators, and private funders.

"In most accounts, new teachers need three or four years to achieve competency and several more to reach proficiency." (Feiman-Nemser 2003). This means placing a major emphasis on quality induction programs in districts supported by state and federal funding, as well as careful attention to first-job placement for these beginners in teams or paired settings where they can be immersed in observing good practice and conversations with experienced practitioners.

This approach to the gradual assumption of professional responsibility may or may not carry significant cost implications, but is unavoidable if we are to improve the quality of instruction on a large scale. The Milken design for differentiated staffing (1999) shows ways to put novice teachers in schools with integrated teams led by master teachers. Even without such models, true team teaching widely adopted and married to quality long-term induction programs could make beginning teachers highly productive in their early career and eliminate the need for full solo responsibility for teaching decisions they were unprepared to make.

There is an influence on what teachers know and can do that may be more powerful than their preparation programs: that is the work environments into which they go when they take their first jobs. The next section of this monograph is about that workplace and its culture – the second "big rock". The argument will be that the critical role in shaping the workplace environment is the one played by leaders, especially the principal. What are the elements of such a professional environment, and why does it count in the equation of growing teaching expertise?

"Overall, if we compared two average students, one in a school with low professional community, and the other in a school with high professional community, the students in the high community would score about 27% higher on the SRS measure. The difference would represent a gain of 31 percentile points."

– Newmann and Wehlage

"Strong professional communities...will typically produce frequent disagreements and disequilibria because they are continually questioning and debating issues of teachers' practice. They are involved in a critical school wide focus on teaching and learning that Little (1990) labels 'joint work.' . . . The ultimate goal is to increase teachers' interpretive power."

"We think a key leadership role in constructing a professional learning community is to make visible and expected a vision for what it means to be a good colleague."

"The type of professional learning communities that we envision are intended to integrate simultaneously a focus on teacher affiliation, teacher learning, and student achievement."

– Toole and Seashore, 2001

"Big Rock" #2: Leadership for Strong Organizational Culture

The most immediate and direct influence on teaching expertise is the workplace of the school itself.[9] Over the last two decades, dozens of articulate writers (see bibliography on Professional Community Building) have called for collegial professional cultures in schools where teachers actively collaborate to share craft knowledge, do lesson study, observe one another, analyze student work and data together and adjust their teaching appropriately. But these cultures are as rare as hens' teeth. The reason is not that we cannot name the practices in these cultures or even show what they look like. The reason is that *we have not prepared our school- based leaders to create the human environment where these practices can thrive.* Thus, the second "big rock" is to explicitly teach leaders the skills for building the relationships and practices that make the improvement of teaching and learning the absolute center of school operations. I believe this is the essence of the concept of Professional Learning Community.

Professional Learning Communities (PLC) that produce student results have *Academic Focus* driven by *Productive Professional Relationships*. Both of these are sustained by *Shared Beliefs* about students, about learning, and about how the adults should operate with one another. The school principal is the key figure, in fact, the indispensable figure in building such an environment for the constant increase of teaching expertise, and thus student learning. It takes teacher leaders as well as a skillful principal to make this PLC grow strong, but without a committed and knowledgeable principal it will not happen at all. So developing skilled principals at building PLC becomes "big rock" two.

This chapter is about the most important ways leaders support and embed teaching expertise in the workplace of the school. The operating qualities of a school as workplace that most influence teaching expertise and its constant improvement are: ACADEMIC FOCUS, SHARED BELIEFS, AND PRODUCTIVE PROFESSIONAL RELATIONSHIPS.

[9] "School culture" and "Professional Learning Community" are the two terms under which these workplace conditions have been studied (see bibliography.)

These three qualities interact constantly to grow the teaching expertise of the staff and directly produce higher student achievement (see fig. 1). It takes a particular kind of leadership to develop these qualities. Thus, the second "big rock" is the leadership that does so; and the priority becomes developing people in leadership positions who know how to grow these attributes of Academic Focus, Shared Beliefs, and Powerful, Productive Relationships.

In the 1990s, powerful research showed beyond question that schools that succeeded for children, especially poor urban children, had strong organizational cultures (see bibliography). As more and more work was done to understand these cultures, they came to be called Professional Learning Communities. Toole and Louis pointed out by using the term Professional Learning Community, "we signify our interest not only in discrete acts of teacher sharing, but also in the establishment of a school wide culture that makes collaboration expected, inclusive, genuine, ongoing, and focused on student outcomes. The term integrates three robust concepts...Professionalism [which means] client centered and knowledge based; and 'learning' which places a high value on teacher professional development; and one that is 'communitarian' [meaning it] emphasizes the personal connection [between staff members]".

All of the nine high poverty, high performing schools in the Department of Education's report "Hope for Urban Education" (Charles A. Dana Center 1999) put particular emphasis daily on developing teachers' knowledge and skills. Some principals spent almost half of their time in direct contact with teachers around improving teaching and learning, and in most cases, *created positions for instructional specialists who did the same.* This is a very important capacity-building move. I highlight it in the list of highest priority action plans for improving low performing schools [p.49].

If we put this research together with the Sanders, et al. studies on the primacy of teachers in accounting for student learning, it allows one to hypothesize that *the reason Professional Learning Communities (PLC) increase student learning is that they produce more good teaching by more teachers more of the time.* Put simply, PLC improves teaching, which improves student results, especially for the least advantaged students. It is, therefore, particularly important to understand what these cultures are like and how they are created. I have worked with Matt King and John D'Auria since the mid-1980s on this question, and together we have developed the following framework.

Figure 1.
The DNA of School Leadership Has Three Elements

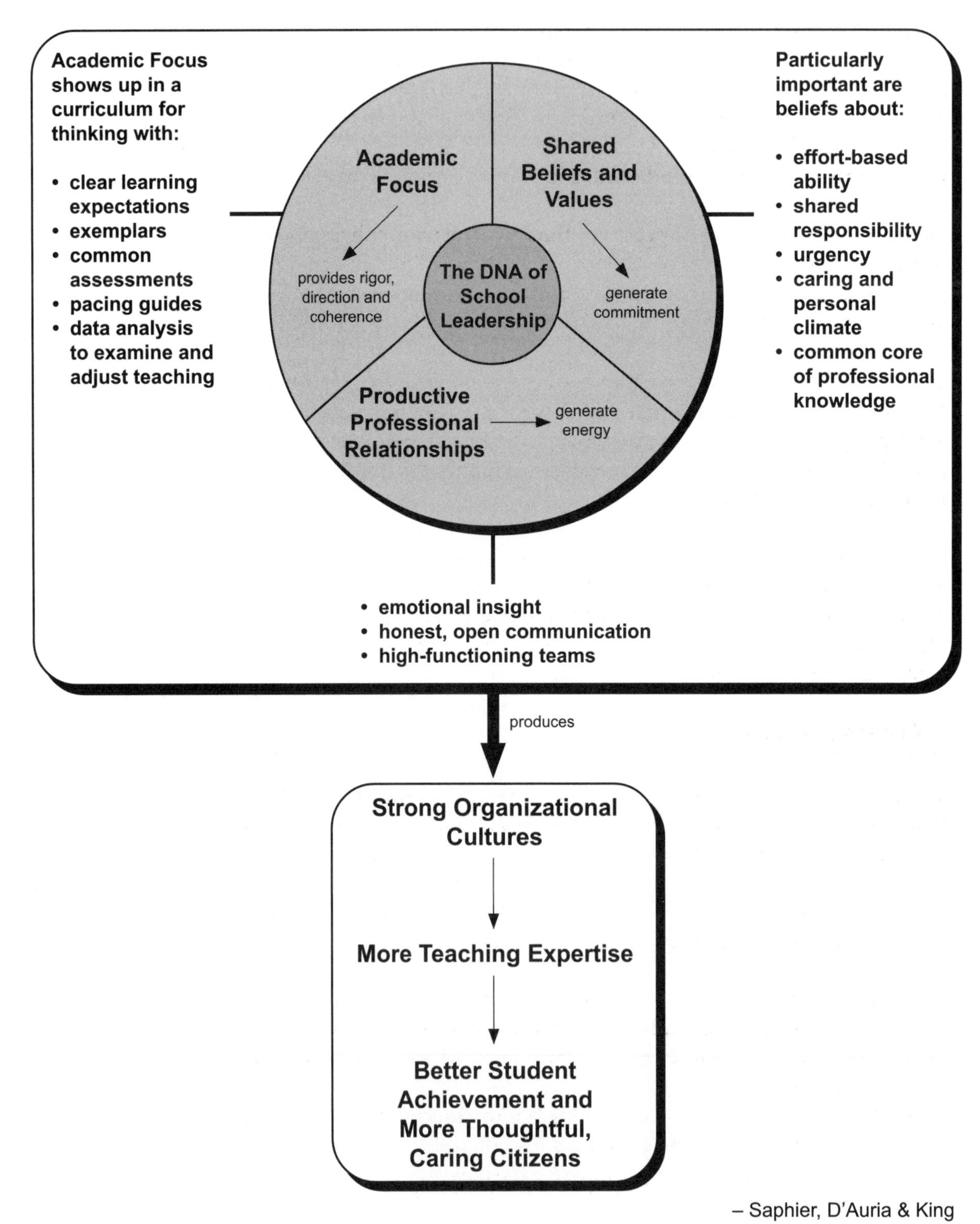

– Saphier, D'Auria & King

Defining the Map of Strong Professional Culture

Excellent schools have Academic Focus, Shared Beliefs, and Productive Professional Relationships. These three are not hierarchical, they are equal; they are not sequential, they are cyclical; they are not causative of one another, they are interactive. Together we think that they form a new and useful way of understanding what Professional Learning Community is and how to build it.

Academic Focus is a set of practices that bring clarity, coherence and precision to everybody's classroom work. It is a "professional" aspect of PLC because it has rigor, precision, alignment, accountability, and data at its center.

Shared Beliefs serve to give people meaning in their work, a feeling of belonging and commitment to one another, and the endurance to keep going when the going gets tough. They are the "community" part of PLC because they forge the commitments and the bonds that keep people together.

Productive Professional Relationships are defined by norms of interaction among staff that enable the honesty, curiosity, and self-examination that lead to better teaching and learning. They are the "learning" part of PLC because they enable and fuel constant teacher learning about the practice of teaching.

I. Academic Focus

The practices of Academic Focus can be grouped into three components, all related to concepts of precision, logic, and organization. And they show up in observable, tangible practices and artifacts.

1. A rigorous, thought-provoking curriculum that is crystal clear because it has the following features:

    - compact list of clear learning expectations for each grade and subject or course ready to hand a newly hired teacher
    - tangible exemplars of student proficiency for each learning expectation
    - "power standards" (Reeves 2002) (i.e., identification of most important high leverage skills)
    - common end-of-course/year assessments with common standards

- common quarterly assessments
- emphasis on non-fiction writing across the content areas
- high level thinking tasks and questions in the learning experiences for students of all academic skill levels. No dumbed down thinking even though students may have low skill levels. [see American Diploma Project]
- materials (guides, manuals, realia, tasks) that support best content specific pedagogy and high level thinking
- pacing guides

It is a fact that most schools in America do not have these practices now. Where parent and community support are strong and family expectations are high, children seem to do fairly well anyway. But a clear and rigorous curriculum with the above bullets tangibly in place is absolutely essential for children of the poor (and would benefit legions of low to mid performing middle class students too.) This is also true of the next two features of "Academic Focus."

2. Systematic Analysis of Data and Feedback Mechanisms to Students
   - classroom systems for high frequency, detailed feedback to students that compare their work with work that meets standards and gives help on how to improve
   - quarterly teacher team meetings to analyze student data from common assessments
   - weekly team meetings to improve instruction of skills and concepts with which students are struggling

3. "Academic Press"
   "Academic Press" means that the faculty and staff press the students to do well, and they do so in multiple ways. Students are consistently sent messages that they are able and that academic achievement is important for them now and in the future. Persistence and pursuit, support and push show up in the students' experience in equal measure.

   The more this commitment is present, the more it shows up in individual teacher behavior, classroom structures and practices, school policies and procedures. For a complete description of these behaviors, practices and policies. See DuFour 2004 and Saphier in DuFour 2005.

Related Terms and Notable Advocates

	Authors	Related Terms in the Literature
"Relationships"	Michael Fullan Phil Schlecty	Collegiality, Experimentation, Honesty, Contact, Joint Work, Appreciation, Collaboration, Courage, Risk-taking, Deprivatising Practice, Non-Defensiveness, Creative Conflict, Initiative
"Academic Focus"	Mike Schmoker Rick DuFour	Data, Precision, Alignment, Assessment, Goals, Proficiency Targets, Accountability, Feedback
"Shared Beliefs"	Tom Sergiovanni Lorraine Monroe Jeff Howard	Shared Responsibility, Community, Effort-Based Ability, Real Knowledge Base, Passion, Urgency, Tenacity, Caring, Resiliency

II. Shared Beliefs

The following Shared Beliefs ripple out into individual teacher behavior, class routines, procedures and practices, and adults' behavior with one another. They also show up in school structures, including schedules, grouping, and grading practices. They are evident in interactive teaching in very concrete and observable ways (Saphier and Gower 1997). They particularly influence the spirit, the fiber, the character and commitment of the staff in the school to be persistent when the going gets tough with discouraged students or youngsters who have fallen behind:

- Effort Based Ability (i.e., "smart is something you can get" (Jeff Howard). "Think you can; Work hard; Get smart." [Verna Ford's personal communication during her years with The Efficacy Institute].

- Errors are normal and opportunities for learning and are simply feedback that enable productive goal setting.
- Care, quality and craftsmanship are what count, not speed or being first or fastest.
- Good students (and professional teachers) know how to ask for help and get critique and feedback on their work.
- Climate counts. Students need to feel known, included, and valued for who they are, and be members of a cohesive supportive community (NRCIM 2003; Poplin and Weeres 1992; Resnick et al. 1997; Sparks 2003).
- The success of our students is our joint responsibility, and when they succeed, it is to our joint credit and a cumulative accomplishment.
- Urgency… "Our school can do a lot better for most of its students than it is doing now. Each child can succeed at an important task every day." (Schlechty 2001)
- There is a real common core of professional knowledge about generic teaching and learning and about content specific pedagogy to which we must be constantly reaching out. It is huge, complex, and organized around repertoire and matching, not singularly "effective" behaviors (Saphier and Gower 1997).

I would like to lift one of these beliefs out for special consideration, "Effort Based Ability". "Malleable intelligence" is another term for this belief. It holds that innate ability is not as deterministic as effort in predicting academic success. This belief asserts that virtually all students have the capacity to achieve proficiency in literacy and numeracy, even if they feel stupid or exhibit low performance now. It is not defective intellectual capacity that sorts our students onto a bell curve. This view of intellectual ability leads directly to the inescapable conclusion that we could actually teach all the children if we had enough diversified tools, and they could be made to believe in their own capacity (and perhaps also if they believed that it would matter for them if they did.)

Put simply, "All the students[10] have sufficient intellectual capacity to do rigorous academic work at high standards." They may come with widely varying levels of performance and preparation, different levels of commitment and motivation, and different rates of learning. Almost none are hampered by defective mental equipment for meeting high standards. It is primarily motivation, the belief in self, and

[10] Except those who may have organic damage of some sort.

the capacity to mobilize effective effort that determines success in school (and in other walks of life, too.) Good teaching with high expectations, of course, can have a powerful impact on these student beliefs.

> Educational leaders need to pay close attention to the prevailing beliefs about intelligence that permeate a school community. Understanding what factors influence children to develop a particular perspective on their intelligence has significant potential for teachers and school leaders. The work of Carol Dweck and her colleagues indicates that the particular view a child has about intelligence will influence the type of goals they establish in school; the amount of effort they expend on learning; and how they will respond to setbacks (see Dweck & Legget 1988). Given the significance of these behaviors, adults who are charged with teaching young people will want to influence children to persevere in the face of obstacles and understand the learning potential of mistakes. Helping students to develop and nurture these habits of mind will aid schools and communities to achieve what Snow and Yallow (1982) refer to as the most important aim of education: aptitude development.
>
> A strong argument can be made that without altering the basic assumption of fixed and unalterable intelligence, all the strategies, educational interventions, initiatives, and innovations that researchers and teachers design to improve schools, particularly in our urban centers, will fail. Without addressing the futile conclusions that flow from this assumption, education can only sort talent rather than develop it (Chapman 1988). Lurking behind failed attempts to help students learn and improve their achievement is the belief that the problem ultimately lies not with the pedagogy or the curriculum or the educational framework but with the immutability of the intellectual deficit within the child, the group, the culture, the gender, the race.
>
> – D'Auria 2001

Resnick (1995), building on the work of Jeff Howard (1990), succinctly captures this problem and points us in the direction of a solution:

> Early in this century, we built an education system around the assumption that aptitude is paramount in learning and that it is largely hereditary. The system was oriented toward selection, distinguishing the naturally able from the less able and providing students with programs thought suitable to their talents. In other periods, most notably during the Great Society reforms, we worked on a compensatory principle, arguing that special effort, by an individual or an institution, could make up for low aptitude. The third possi-

> bility-that effort actually creates ability, that people can become smart by working hard at the right kinds of learning tasks-has never been taken seriously in America or indeed in any European society, although it is the guiding assumption of education institutions in societies with a Confucian tradition.
>
> – Resnick 1995, pp. 55-62

Wide faculty acceptance of this belief that one can "get smarter," coupled with clear and demanding proficiency targets and periodic assessments, leads to what Newmann and Wehlage (1995) call "academic press" for all students, that is, the persistent push for quality

"Proficiency" is a central concept to improving student performance and offering equal opportunity to all our children. It is also a central idea of the standards movement. "Proficiency" means the standard of work which we define as a high and rigorous level of performance or mastery. It is a "3" on a 4-point scale, 4 being "accomplished" or "above standard." Anything below this level is not OK, not finished. Anything over it is OK, is acceptable. At this level of performance we are satisfied. This standard of "proficiency" is objective, independent of students, their backgrounds or what we think is reasonable for "these kids."

The point is that our work is not done, either as students or as teachers, until this standard is reached. The concept of "proficiency" thus embeds the commitment to get all students to this level, even if some take much longer to get there. This is a very different idea about schooling, because it is unwilling to passively allow the supposed "bell curve of ability" to become a self-fulfilling prophecy for student results.

A related concept is an "exemplar," which is a real piece of student work that demonstrates "proficiency" (e.g. a writing sample, a word problem that has been solved, a reading passage with questions to answer and the answers written out, a completed essay that meets criteria). Not only do we and the students have the example of "proficiency" to look at, but we also have a list of the criteria that the sample embodies. In addition, we have something to guide us to be able to see how and where the criteria are met in the work sample, perhaps a rubric for discriminating levels of performance above and below "proficiency". Other terms used for the above are "proficiency target," "anchor paper," and "benchmark student performance."

Schools and teachers committed to "proficiency" usually generate common end-of-course or year assessments. This is a set of problems, questions, writing prompts, etc. that are created and given to students to elicit performances. (Sometimes in service of clarity of expectations, they are given to students at the beginning of the year or course.) The products the students produce on these common assessments are compared to the exemplars of "proficiency" described above. What each student produces is used to "grade" the student's current level of performance in relation to "proficiency." These assessments themselves, based on a common image of "proficiency," become common across the whole school district when there is a commitment to elevating all students' achievement.

work from all students and the expressed belief that all can attain it. The attitude is: We do not expect all students to learn at the same rate or meet standards at the same time, especially when they have wide differences in their prior preparation. We can take it as our responsibility to teach our kids to believe in themselves and also to teach them how to work not just harder but smarter, with appropriate strategies. This only makes sense since thorough reviews of the history of IQ (Gould 1981 and 1996) coupled with studies of the role or "hard wired ability" in academic and workplace success (Perkins 1995) have discredited IQ as fixed and deterministic of student success.

This belief also leads to a different conception of error. Mistakes are normal, to be expected. And mistakes are not proof of low intelligence but opportunities for learning. Thus, instead of avoiding mistakes or covering them up, mistakes become an accepted part of learning. This belief, it turns out, plays just as important a part in open communication between adults as it does in the learning environment of students. Belief in "developed" capacity for a school and its practitioners becomes a pillar of the Professional Learning Community itself.

Since most of us in this country were brought up to believe in the bell curve of intellectual ability, it is significant work for a leader to address this belief system with a faculty. This work involves much introspection, conversation, and modeling. But the slowness of beliefs to change does not prevent a school from instituting policies and practices at the school level that are consistent with the belief that "smart is something you can get," and effective effort is the main determinant of success. These structures, policies, and practices are then becomes major topics of study for those working on school leadership. I have written elsewhere in detail about these policies and procedures (Saphier in DuFour 2005).

III. Productive Professional Relationships

"Relationships, relationships, relationships – it's all about relationships." Tony Alvarado said this in his early days of leadership in New York's District #2. What characterizes these relationships?

In schools that grow teaching expertise, relationships between adults actively show 12 norms[11]:

[11] Matt King and I identified a similar set 20 years ago (Saphier and King 1985.) Though some items have been modified to reflect current research, the overall importance of these aspects of human relationships in schools have been reaffirmed by the research of the 90s (see bibliography on PLC.)

Relationships

12 Cultural Norms of Professional Community

The sine qua non . . . Requisite norms that allow all the others to develop	What "Collaboration" really means: norms which lead directly to improved instruction and better student achievement	Important background norms that generate affiliation and commitment
1 Honest, Open Communication	**4 Systematic Examination of Data**	**8 Protecting What's Important**
2 Involvement in Decision Making	**5 Non-Defensive Self Examination of Teaching Practice** 5 elements of collegiality	**9 Respect & Confidence**
3 Distributed Leadership & Initiative	**6 Reaching Out to the Knowledge Base**	**10 Appreciation & Recognition**
	7 Experimentation, Analysis, & Self Critique in Groups sharing, listening, & encouraging	**11 Celebration, Caring, Humor, Traditions, Rituals, & Ceremonies**
	Groups of teachers who share students and/or content demonstrate these behaviors in regular meetings. They align curriculum, standards, and assessment and constantly examine student work to improve lessons and make student tasks more interesting and focused.	**12 High Expectations & Accountability for Adults**

Research for Better Teaching, Inc. and *TEACHERS*[21]

- honest, open communication that allows equanimity with conflict and disagreement; supports robust, healthy professional dialog and the ability to discuss the undiscussable
- legitimate decision-making and involvement
- distributed instructional leadership and initiative to do something for the good of the school or team
- habits of systematic examination of data
- non-defensive self-examination of practice
- curiosity and constant learning from the knowledge base on teaching and learning
- experimentation, analysis, and critique in groups leading to deprivatization of teaching practice
- protecting what is important
- respect and confidence
- appreciation and recognition
- celebration, caring, humor, traditions, rituals and ceremonies that bind the adults into a community
- willingness to hold each other accountable for agreed norms and student results.

The above items shape a human environment for adults (with, of course, perceivable consequences in the environment for children). It is a human environment where people feel safe yet challenged; where they feel a sense of belonging and ownership; and where people roll out of bed early in the morning and look forward to going to work. This is different from the precision and rigor that comes from the Academic Focus factors and different from the passion and drive that comes from the Shared Belief factors. These Relationship elements enable challenge and synergy between people. They are far more than "feel good" traits. They enable the courageous conversations that maximize learning and continuous improvement of teaching expertise.

IV. Student Culture of Pride, Aspiration and Respect

In successful schools for disadvantaged children, the staff pays serious and planful attention to the student culture. Expertise at building student motivation to learn shows up not only in individual teacher behavior, but also in school-wide policies and practices that shape the answers to the following questions:

EFFORT — Does the social system of the school and the student culture make it embarrassing or "uncool" for a youngster to be seen working hard on academics and doing well, or is academic effort supported and celebrated among the students?

PRIDE — Do students see their school as a place for "losers" and distance themselves from it, or do they feel a sense of belonging and exert themselves to make "their" school look good?

BETTER LIFE — Do the students see school as a place to "get through" and focus their energy on socializing with friends, or do they have a vision of a better life attainable through academic achievement?

RESPECT — Do the students feel contained and coerced by the environment, or do they feel valued and included in shaping decisions about the life of the school?

KNOWN AND CARED FOR — Do the students feel anonymous or are they known and cared for by multiple adults in the school?

I have not included the arena of "student culture" in the DNA diagram on p. 24, but for many schools, especially inner city secondary schools for children of poverty, this is a vital topic for leaders. I observed this first hand over the seven years my RBT colleagues and I participated in the Phoenix-like rise of the Jeremiah Burke HS in Dorchester, MA between 1995 and 2002. Deliberately building a student culture of pride, aspiration, and respect was crucial to the results Dr. Stephen Leonard and his staff achieved. From a gang-ruled, chaotic, and dangerous school in a decrepit building that had lost its high school accreditation (unheard of in recent MA history,) Burke went to being a school where every one of the 200+ graduating seniors was accepted to college or jr. college. That story is a textbook case for the DNA elements described here [Academic Focus, Shared Beliefs, Productive Professional Relationships.] But in addition, the Burke staff focused unceasing attention on shaping student attitudes about academic work and about school as a place worthy of student affiliation and identify.

There is much justifiable emphasis these days on the importance of students feeling known and valued by adults in their school. The focus is on each individual student feeling known. I am writing here about something different: the *student culture* and what it authorizes and, more, encourages in student norms and mores. The point is that adults can influence and shape that student culture into one that celebrates being a good student. Without taking that on explicitly in secondary schools, the predominant teen culture of music, media, consumerism, and hanging out with friends easily trumps investment in achievement. Pride in the school, aspiration for a better life through education, and valuing academic effort can become the hallmarks of the student culture if the adults take it on with the same seriousness and commitment we are bringing to analyzing data on student results. I have seen this repeatedly in inner city schools that are outperforming the stereotypes of what their students "should" be able to do.

Roles of Leaders and Teams

Robust dialog and non-defensiveness between teachers are grounded in a leader's willingness to be open about discomfort and non-defensive about the examination of practice—and being so in the presence of others. True confessions? No. But true thinking out loud and honest sharing of confusions and disappointment as well as satisfaction? Yes. When groups of teachers bring this quality to the table, we get the next level of professional talk: joint commitments to experiment with new approaches, to analyze what the teaching is doing for student learning, and willingness to critique our efforts together. Colleagues disagree without jeopardizing their relationships; tenderness and hypersensitivity to criticism dissolve into the challenge and stimulation of friendly debate. That is when the promise of "collegiality" really flowers—and when teachers feel the satisfaction of growing and learning together in a flourishing professional community.

> The kind of conversation that promotes teacher learning differs from usual modes of teacher talk, which feature personal anecdotes and opinions and are governed by norms of politeness and consensus. What distinguishes professional learning communities from support groups where teachers mainly share ideas and offer encouragement is their *critical stance and commitment to inquiry.* Exercising what Lord (1994) calls the traits of critical colleagueship, teachers ask probing questions, invite colleagues to observe, and review their teaching and their students' learning and hold out ideas for discussion and debate. Among critical colleagues, disagreements are viewed as opportunities to consider different perspectives and clarify beliefs, not something to be avoided.
>
> – Sharon Feiman-Nemser, 2001

Our case here is that the emotional intelligence of leaders and team members is the indispensable catalyst to develop this critical stance. How do we create conditions for these courageous conversations?

Certain structures are necessary to bring people together often enough to have growth oriented conversations: designated groups that build agreements about common curriculum; structures of time and intent that increase contact and dialog for professional purposes between staff; procedures and support for being in each other's classrooms to see what people are doing; protocols for how to talk about the visits with focus afterwards. We can have all these elements present, however, and still hear conversations that sidestep tough issues and tiptoe through the tulips; we are making "nice" not making professional community; we are avoiding disagreement and conflict and not using emotional intelligence.

The breakthrough into the kind of courageous conversations we are talking about is facilitated when people bring student work to the table for examination with peers. The concreteness of those work samples generates questions; these conversations set the platform for the dialog and the agendas for experimentation in one's teaching. To get the juices flowing, we need some explicit discussion of norms[12] for how we will act with one another; we need the leadership of group members who are willing to model being vulnerable. These are people who will share their unresolved problems and questions, and similarly challenge their colleagues to do the same (Hiebert, et al.2002).

A number of skills support these interactions—active listening, problem finding, brainstorming, group norm setting, giving feedback, and facilitating. Training can be provided for all of these and will be helpful. (Keiffer-Barone and Ware 2002). *But nothing will be as helpful as group members who are willing to model self-awareness, self-examination, experimentation and risk-taking with colleagues.* Nothing can set the tone for this better than building-based leaders who will do the same, such as principals, assistant principals, department chairs, specialists and support teachers of all kinds. They must be willing to advocate and model all these qualities in the conduct of their own daily business. Along with modeling must come explicit school and district commitment to these norms and deliberate use of them in hiring and induction of new teachers.

[12] Norms such as no "put-downs", a place for everyone's voice, stick to agenda, start on time, etc.

At a still deeper level of these relationships is the capacity to manage conflict with emotional intelligence. This can be the pivot for all the rest. Day after day in schools across America, change initiatives, instructional improvement, and better results for children are blocked, sabotaged, or killed through silence and inaction. In our work with school and district-based leaders, my colleagues John D'Auria, Matt King and I have often noticed that this lack of follow-through results from the avoidance or inability to face conflict openly and make it a creative source of energy among educators. This in turn derives from the underdeveloped "emotional intelligence" of leaders (Goleman 1999). The ability to read first one's own and others' feelings is essential to the work of change, especially in workplaces that are as loosely managed as schools. So we have elevated this aspect of leadership out for special treatment in our courses and coaching work. It lays the foundation for the changes and progressive development in the Professional Learning Community.

We are taking the position that a vital aspect of leadership is to help expose conflict and view it as the engine of creativity and learning. Successful leaders get "people on the executive team to listen to and learn from one another." Leaders who do this realize that conflict left uncovered will fester anyway. "A leader has to have the emotional capacity to tolerate uncertainty, frustration, and pain . . . he or she has to raise tough questions without getting too anxious." Such leaders can "cook the conflict" so the pot doesn't boil over, but the issue stays on everyone's front burner at an acceptable level of anxiety. This is because such leaders know that solutions to challenging problems "lie in the collective intelligence of employees at all levels, who need to use one another as resources, often across boundaries, and learn their way to those solutions" (Heifitz and Laurie 2001). Leaders must learn how to make the undiscussable discussable (Barth 2002).

Academic focus, shared beliefs, and the powerful, productive relationships weave together in the warp and weft of how adults behave with one other and with students, how they plan, and how they reflect. These three qualities and the practices that go with them become built into the operations of the whole school, into the talk between educators as they conduct daily business, and most particularly, into the operation of teams of teachers who share students or content. You can see and hear the three qualities (or their absence) simultaneously at a team meeting. For important evidence of a school that is improving student achievement, look at teams, their talk, their staffing and their access:

- teams of teachers who share students or content, how they interact, what they do with their time
- talk and modus operandi of the team leaders who work with teachers directly and in groups
- access and reaching out to the Common Core of Professional Knowledge about Teaching and Learning (Appendix A)

They also become built into the way a building's instructional leaders (call them coaches, staff developers, directors, or department chairs) talk with individual teachers and groups of teachers. (See Appendix B) These conversations, of course, are dependent on the building being staffed so that there are *enough trained instructional leaders to cause all the teachers to have frequent high quality conversations about their teaching practices and their results with students, leading to observation and critique of one another's practice.*

Implications for Building Effective Professional Learning Communities

It is the central job of school leadership, especially the principal and supporting central office staff, to build the three qualities of Academic Focus, Shared Beliefs, and Powerful, Productive Relationships into the fabric of the school, its people, and their practices and their organization.

If you take the principal and other key building leaders out of the picture as a committed and skillful force for these qualities, then no successful PLC will form. The possibilities of all other forces combined (state education law and policy, standardized testing and accountability, central office staff development, parent and community pressure) to raise student achievement are fatally weakened.

The prime influence on the knowledge and skills of building-based leaders to grow these qualities is the central office by its: (a) recruiting and hiring of leaders; (b) supervision and evaluation of leaders; and (c) support and staff development of leaders. Leadership must start at the top. The prime determinants on how much energy the central office puts into developing building leadership are the commitment and priorities of the superintendent and top administrators to do so.

••••••••••••••••••••••••••••••••

Let us pause for a moment to consider the role of supervision and evaluation in improving teaching and what leaders do to carry out this function.

Very few schools have adequate infrastructure (read as sufficient personnel) to make teacher evaluation serve as an effective vehicle for improving instruction. Because of the hectic and unpredictable workload of school administrators, evaluation is too infrequent and often too superficial to have much impact on teacher learning. The best of administrators do make good use of the sparse quality time they get with each of their teachers in an evaluation cycle. They observe and analyze well, and they have productive conferences. In addition, they make frequent 15-minute visits to classrooms and have short, useful conversations with many teachers entirely aside from evaluation. But this is still not enough. Therefore, the improvement of teaching, which can be aided by good evaluation, must rely on other systems.

The complexity of teaching requires that we put in place in each school district an infrastructure of people who are instructional experts. They are building-based and available full-time to work: with beginning teachers on learning how to teach, with experienced teachers on how to teach their content better, and with all teachers on how to deal with problems and pursue their goals for instructional improvement. This infrastructure cannot be developed through attending only to better teacher evaluation; it must also create new mechanisms for supervision. So let us separate conceptually the processes for supervision from those of evaluation.

Let us agree that the purpose of teacher evaluation shall be to maintain high, minimum standards of teacher performance. Make sure no one falls below the line of proficient performance; make sure that the line is high; ensure that children will not be damaged or be victims of malpractice through incompetence.[13]

In contrast, the purpose of supervision is the improvement of instruction. It is not thc only vehicle, but it is a powerful one, and is substantially undeveloped in most schools. Supervision means receiving high

[13] This is no small feat, requiring skill, courage, and central office back-up. Elsewhere (Saphier 1993) I have described the procedures, the forms, and the political process to create a teacher evaluation system that accomplishes the separation of supervision and evaluation. These are evaluation systems that put the emphasis squarely on professional growth, evaluation systems that can also be fair, humane, and decisive in dealing with poor teaching.

quality feedback from someone who knows what they are talking about. Supervision means engaging in challenging and data-based dialog about one's teaching decisions with another educator. And supervision means having someone you can rely on for honest, supportive questioning and problem solving.

So let us put a "Staff Development Teacher" in each school (Montgomery County, MD); or put a "Director of Instruction" who is part of the administrators' unit in each K-8 school (Boston, MA); or put a "coach" in literacy and mathematics in every building (New York City); or give special training to an assistant principal and make sure they spend 80% of their time in classes with teachers. It does not matter so much what these supervisory positions are called: match the title to the culture. It does matter that they be very good at their work. It does matter that they have professional expertise at using, articulating, and at observing and analyzing for the items in the common core of professional knowledge. It particularly matters that the culture of the school be highly developed around honesty, openness, inquiry, and constant professional growth. Thus, for the principal it means ensuring constant attention to this culture. No one else can shepherd the effort (though all must contribute to it). No one else can make sure the instructional specialists I have been writing about here are deployed well and operate efficiently.

This profile of Professional Learning Community implies three different kinds of leadership, and none of us can be equally adept at all three: (1) drivers of academic focus, (2) spiritual leaders with shared beliefs, and (3) leaders who display developed emotional intelligence for building powerful, productive professional relationships. Leaders need to be aware that all three are necessary and need to find others in their communities to complement their strengths and fill in for their weaknesses. Without attention to all three qualities, cultures of improvement are incomplete, and gains will not endure.

Academic Focus and Shared Beliefs without Productive Relationships will be hollow and vulnerable. The elements of commitment will reside in the rhetoric and perhaps even the behavior of the devoted few, but will not spread across the faculty without the right Relationships.

Shared Beliefs and Productive Relationships without Academic Focus will fall short because we are not sure where to aim our efforts and probably will not even be aiming at the same targets.

Productive Relationships and Focus without Shared Beliefs will not produce the energy and staying power to work in difficult situations, in inner cities, and with our most needy children.

Our work is educating all our students to be good citizens who reach proficiency targets with academic skills . . . *all* our students. "Leave no child behind" says our most recent education reform law. We need powerful organizations to do that. So let us design our school improvement efforts around Academic Focus, Shared Beliefs, and Productive Relationships, all supported by emotional intelligence.

If this is the right cast for what school culture is, (or its 21st century update, Professional Learning Community) then we need to act on it. We already know that schools with strong Professional Learning Communities improve instruction rapidly and thus get better student results. Building and strengthening these features of the school organization and its human environment constitutes the main job of leadership. Therefore, the education, certification, and evaluation of leaders must be designed around how to lead in this way — the knowledge and skills of cultural leadership. A good map of the components is the starting point. That is the point of this second "big rock".

Building Professional Learning Community is not work for the faint of heart or for those who seek simple answers. It is not the work of heroes either. Heroes have their place but we do not need more of them just now. We need more full-hearted people who are willing to be honest with one another and learn from their mistakes—determined people who will band together to believe in children and in their own capacity to reach them.

Now on to our final "rock"—what we must do to make the profession attractive and competitive enough to attract and retain able people.

"Big Rock" #3: Higher Salaries and Differentiated Career Paths for Teachers

One main reason for the low level of teaching expertise is that good people in teaching do not stay in the classroom long enough to acquire the necessary professional and practical knowledge. Many who do manage to acquire it leave anyway after a few years because they cannot afford to stay. An American practicing in a demanding knowledge-based profession with five years of experience deserves to make $70,000 a year if he/she is performing at a high level and getting results for clients. But $38,000 is what an experienced teacher with a spouse and two young children will likely make in an American city. Most idealistic, skilled, effective young people who consider teaching never enter at all because they see the economic handwriting on the wall.

Matthew Miller (2004) makes the case for raising teacher salaries by half for staff serving disadvantaged children, and by half again for those who are most effective. Tony Milanowski's (2003) survey data shows that such a raise is about what it would take to attract today's college graduates into teaching as a career. Miller shows that the national price tag would be $30 billion annually, which is only a 7% increase in K-12 spending. That is one-quarter of our current annual expenditures in Iraq; only 1.4% of our normal federal budget (U.S. Federal Government Budget 2003); half what we spend on pornography (Federal Reserve Bank of Minneapolis 2000) and gambling (Forester Research, Cambridge 1998; American Gaming Association 2003). This investment would make a tremendous *life difference* to a huge number of our children and produce positive ripple effects to our entire population.

Current adminstration proposals, to eliminate the estate tax, cost about $30 billion (Miller 2005). Why not trade this gift to the wealthy for revolutionizing the conditions of teaching?

In addition to salaries, a career path for service at the building level that promises increased responsibility for instructional leadership and further salary for that increased responsibility would make a significant difference in recruitment and retention (Milken 1999; Wise 2004).

This third "big rock" of higher salaries and differentiated career path for teachers will help pull the capable people we need into teaching. It will end the revolving door of personnel in schools for poor children that so hampers our improvement efforts now. Paying teachers and school leaders competitive wages will not, of course, by itself, ensure good education for all our children. Attracting more educated and ambitious people into the profession will not automatically create good teachers or good leaders. We still need the solid focus on expertise argued in an earlier section. However, without this national commitment to increasing salaries for teachers, all our other efforts are consigned to produce slow-motion and small-scale changes. We will continue to have small numbers of extraordinary schools created by dedicated individuals in high poverty areas. They have been discovered in every corner of our nation whenever researchers have sought them out from Ron Edmonds (1978) through the 2004 study of high performing high schools (NASSP 2004): schools that erupt into brilliance and fade from the scene because the infrastructure of expertise and leadership is not there to sustain them. *To bring this effort to scale across the nation requires more good teaching than the current unequal system will ever create by itself.*

"There are probably a hundred things we need to do for these [low performing] schools, and 10 big things that could make a difference, but if you could focus on only one thing, the most important would be teacher quality. The teacher question is so vital that the Hart-Rudman Commission, the same group whose report presciently stressed America's vulnerability to major terror attacks, defined teacher quality as an issue of *national security*. ...With research showing that half the achievement gap facing poor children is due not to poverty or family conditions, but to systematic differences in teacher quality, the question of teacher recruitment in poor schools is more than just the biggest issue in education. It's the next frontier for social justice." (Miller 2004)

Raising salaries in the manner proposed here calls for a performance-based system for evaluating teachers, connected to student results, but not tied to a numbers game of standardized test scores or so output-oriented that it oversimplifies the incredible complexity of interactive teaching (Saphier, Simon and Weast in Essay 3).

Matthew Miller's proposal for raising the salaries of teachers in poor communities is spelled out in detail in his article in American Educator (2004). "The federal government would raise salaries for every teacher in poor schools in America by *50 percent*. But this offer would be conditioned on two fundamental reforms. First, teachers and their unions would have to agree to raise the pay of the top half of performers in the teacher corps (and those in shortage specialties) *another 50 percent on average*. Second, the unions would have to streamline the dismissal process for poor performing teachers to a fair, swift, four-to-six month period."

The salary raises for high performing teachers would not be simply "merit pay" tied to student achievement. Accomplished teachers would be in charge of the instructional program for teams of their colleagues. A lead teacher "would lead the team with the assistance of another senior colleague. Other members of the team would include two novice teachers who intend to commit themselves to a teaching career; two under-prepared teachers, who want to serve but may not be committed to teaching as a career; and six half-time student teachers who are completing teacher preparation. The team would also include four interns who work half time for half pay as they conclude their initial preparation to teach." (Wise 2004)

Lowell Milken's model (1999) has two master teachers ($70,000 per annum) in an elementary school that was formerly staffed by 24 regular classroom teachers. These master teachers teach children 10 hours a week and spend the rest of their time facilitating curriculum development, leading staff development, conducting peer feedback, and doing demonstration lessons.

Twelve mentor teachers ($30-60,000 per annum) are in charge of small clusters of associate teachers with whom they team teach. They collaborate with colleagues to develop benchmark lessons and observe and provide peer assistance for colleagues.

Twelve associate teachers ($25-35,000) are early career teachers who have full-time teaching responsibilities under the supervision of the mentor teachers with whom they often do side-by-side teaching.

Twelve paraprofessionals ($15- 21,000) work in the classes under the direction of associate and mentor teachers.

Milken's differentiated staffing plan does not actually raise dollar cost for the elementary school profiled at all. However, he needs to join his proposal to Miller's (2004) to create a career path desirable enough to retain the energetic and the able in the profession.

The system could be phased in only for new hires in districts, with currently employed teachers continuing to work till retirement under the terms of their old contract if they so desired, but eligible for the new arrangement (which, of course, many would choose.) This two-tiered system would smooth transition issues but work rapidly, given the current turnover of teachers in poor areas.

I want to emphasize that raising salaries is a background condition for improving teaching, not a pathway for doing it. The development of widespread teaching expertise in a school district requires an infrastructure of human resources that is currently absent from most districts' planning, staffing, or budgeting. The average professional development budget in American school districts is under 1% of total personnel expenditures, which is, of course, ridiculous by industry standards of 7 to 10%. How in these circumstances could any school organization be an engine for improved teaching and learning?

Therefore, budgets for development of personnel must rise at least to the 5% level. The one urban district that sustained such expenditures over an eight-year period was District #2 in New York City. Connecticut did so over fifteen years. Both are the two shining examples in the nation that showed improved achievement of urban children (Elmore 1999; Darling-Hammond 1996).

Implications of Higher Salaries and Professional Standards

The implications for professionalization of teaching are profound. With this kind of money going into salaries and staff development, public pressure for knowledge-based teacher education and certification would be irresistible. Independent licensing boards would be called for to fairly uphold high standards of entry into the profession. Teaching would become an eleven-month job with an eight-hour day on site, thus allowing for much more job embedded professional development time. And teacher evaluation within school districts would have to be both knowledge-based and tied to student performance in some responsible way.

Essay 3 will describe what such a teacher evaluation system looks like, drawing on the four years of work and three years of refinement that have gone into creating a Professional Growth Cycle in Montgomery County, MD. This cycle has formal evaluation as an embedded element of a system that emphasizes professional growth and a focus on student achievement. It includes knowledge-based performance review of teacher behavior and examination of student results in a responsible way. And it was developed from scratch with a close and high functioning Union / School District partnership.

Raising educators' salaries on a significant scale and differentiating instructional leadership positions will take years of coalition building and a return to the moral conscience of our social contract. The world view of John Adams and our other founding fathers blended individualism and freedom with community and fairness to one's neighbors. We need to reawaken that conscience to get the policy changes and commitment that will produce a good education system for our urban and rural poor.

We also need to show how doing so is much less expensive than letting a two-tiered school system continue: one for the affluent and one for the poor. For example, currently the support for a prisoner in American jails costs on average $30,000 per year. Our prison population is two million. That is 60 billion dollars a year and is double the level we spent in 1980 when we had one million prisoners. Given the strong correlation of incarceration to elementary reading level, it would seem that an educated citizenry could reduce this prison expenditure significantly. It would certainly reduce the additional $80 billion a year that US industry spends to develop basic literacy skills in its employees!

Well documented is that poor children's schools are underfunded to meet the needs of their higher English Language Learner and Special Education populations and that their teachers earn less while working in less supportive environments (Hancock vs. Driscoll 2004). This is, indeed, inequality. No wonder our poor children remain behind and their upward mobility remains stifled.

The job is not only to gain public attention and acceptance of the impressive impacts of expertise in teaching but also to convince the economically comfortable that it is in their interest to pay for teaching expertise for other people's children, including poor children. That is not an easy sell. We have to make the case that the jobs, the lifestyle, and the standard of living of the affluent depends in real ways on better education for our least advantaged students. Therefore, it is incumbent on all of us in the educational community to deal more directly with business groups in each state and with legislators at the state and national levels. We have to organize non-profit advocacy groups and through them, reach out to our major foundations like Carnegie, Broad, Rockefeller, Gates and so many others who want to leave a positive mark on the national landscape. They are doing a great deal of good, but they are not focused enough on the essential "big rocks" for education reform.

People are selfish and generous at the same time, as well as brave and fearful. We are all inclined simultaneously to live in our own small, protected worlds and to reach out to the needy only if we can see them. It is up to us to bring out these generous sides of our fellow citizens. It is up to us to keep the moral possibilities before our policy makers so that they, the voting public, and beyond them, the powerful, the wealthy, the influential can reach into their best selves to rectify the imbalances in education so as to sustain our democracy.

While the years pass, those of us within education in policy and leadership roles must continue to act with the resources we have *now* to make significant progress on getting the first two "big rocks" of teaching expertise and strong leadership into the jar. We can do so in our own workplaces, our own districts, states, and colleges. No school, district or city has to wait for salaries to rise in order to build teaching and leadership expertise that can get results for children right now.

Afterword: Practical Note to School Leaders for Implementation

This monograph is aimed first at policy makers and high level leadership teams within school districts because it calls for prioritizing and focusing resources on the things that my colleagues and I at Research for Better Teaching and Teachers 21 feel are most important. It is an argument, a polemic, an attempt to persuade. Thus, it is not a "how to" piece. In our training and consulting work, we deal every day with leaders in schools directly on the "how to's" all the way from building courageous conversations and robust dialog into team meetings to "cleaning up the streets" in a secondary school. Our repertoire around these wide-ranging issues has been informed and enlarged by the many skillful leaders we have worked with over the past 30 years.

Whenever one lays out the "Big Picture" of a complex problem (and improving a school for poor and underperforming children is indeed a complex problem), the number of variables can be overwhelming. It has been our experience that a leader needs a short list of places to focus—a small number of project centers on which to hang the practices and structures outlined above in order to feel a sense of direction and be able to manage the complexity of moving an institution forward. "Academic Focus, Shared Beliefs, and Powerful, Productive Relationships" are conceptual categories for holding big ideas, not concrete projects to work on.

"Teams that work and work on important things" is a project center. And it suggests specific actions (e.g., observe teams and give feedback to team leaders; teach them about agendas and good meeting practices; give them the task of creating common assessments; do a study group for team leaders on courageous conversations; make arrangements for quarterly retreats where teams analyze student data; bring in staff development on analyzing students results in simple yet powerful ways; and ask one team to pilot a "lesson study").

You can see how working on effective teams becomes a project center that enables the principal to work on all three qualities of the Professional Learning Community (See Appendix B). Without adequately developed interpersonal skills and emotional intelligence, the principal will not get too far in this "project center". Thus, we see once again, the significance of educating leaders in how to build powerful, productive relationships, have robust dialog, and build the confidence and interpersonal skills of others.

What follows are recommendations for the dozen or so highest leverage project centers for a school leader. This particular list of priorities comes from 30 years of making these choices with leaders in various districts, and a track record of excellent success in some districts with continuity and staying power in their leadership.

Priority Action Plans for School Improvement

Teaching Expertise

Improve the teaching expertise of all the teachers.

- Embed systematic and continual learning from the **common core of professional knowledge** — and a common language for talking about it — in teacher induction, evaluation, supervision, and professional development.
- **Organize the management of the whole district around adult development** based on the common core of professional knowledge about teaching and learning, since that is the key to increasing student achievement.
- Grow an **infrastructure of expert building–based instructional leaders** who spend most of their time with teachers on examining practice in relation to student learning.

High-functioning Teams

- Develop high-functioning operational teams that *work* (i.e., that operate fluently with trust, conflict, commitment, accountability for each other, and focus on results) and that *work on important things like:*
  - using common assessments and exemplars of proficiency
  - doing detailed analysis of quarterly assessments
  - deprivatizing practice and conducting weekly examination of teaching and learning together
  - supporting aligned and accessible curriculum materials.
  - making annual SMART goals for improving student achievement

- Develop the **emotional intelligence** of the principal and leadership team in each building along with their capacity for **courageous conversations, academic focus and shared beliefs.**
- Generate **urgency** and commitment that virtually **all students shall** achieve proficiency.
- Build **"effort-based ability"** into classroom practices and school structures.

Student Culture

- [Secondary schools] **Clean up the street culture.**
- Build a sense of **identity and pride** in belonging to this school.
- Build relationships where all students are **known and valued**.
- Build a **peer culture that values academic achievement.**
- Ensure well-developed systems for student **support of needy kids and a safety net for the highest need students.**
- Develop programs that show students **images of a better life through education** and nurture **hope** and effort.

Resources and Partnerships

- With **union-management partnership**, develop **school board support** for the centrality of expertise in leadership, teaching and learning, and clarity about the distinction between policy, monitoring, and micromanagement.
- Provide adequate resources for small class sizes where it matters and **reasonable class loads** at secondary levels.
- Maintain **continuity of leadership** in key positions for 5-7 years.

Appendix A: The Tasks of Teaching

The section immediately below summarizes the major findings for the tasks of teaching in generic pedagogy known to impact student learning. These are field-tested, research-validated tasks; and attention to many of them is missing in action from the preparation and evaluation of the majority of practicing teachers in the country.

I. Planning

A teacher carrying out the planning job well for daily lessons makes sure that:

- he/she clearly understands and, thus, can articulate the learning objective in terms of student performance and how it is appropriate for the curriculum and for the students.
- the lessons are designed around big ideas[14] that are important. The students know what these big ideas are. The learning tasks are logically connected to the ideas (Wiggins and McTighe 1998).
- the students have adequate prior knowledge and skills to engage the current learning tasks (Alexander, Editor 1996). Thus, the teacher frequently analyzes her own classroom assessment data to find out which students do and which don't have adequate readiness. She also analyzes her learning materials and texts to identify assumptions of prior knowledge that students may not have.[15]
- the students have enough time to learn the material (Bloom 1968; Carroll 1963).
- the students have materials (displays, examples, manipulatives, texts) that make the learning accessible and do so in multiple ways.

[14] A Big Idea like "A just society balances individual freedom and the common good." Good 21st century curricula for all subjects, even beginning reading and elementary mathematics, start from clear statements of big ideas (Wiggins and McTighe 1998).

[15] For example, to understand in a text: "satellite state to the Soviet Union," students need to understand the general concept that a dominating country can have controlling influence over the decisions of another subservient country's government. Thus, the subservient country is a "satellite" of the dominating country. But in parallel, one needs to understand the vocabulary word "satellite." Understanding what "Prior Knowledge" is needed is another way to describe this relationship. This is knowledge that a teacher can use to predict, prevent, or understand student confusions.

- the teacher anticipates student misconceptions and takes steps to prevent them. (Eaton et al. 1984; Eylon and Linn 1988).
- the students know what good work on the task/assignment would look like [criteria; exemplars] (Frederiksen and White 1997).
- what the students are doing [the activity] could logically be expected to lead them to learn the intended learning [not as obvious as it seems.]
- the intended learning is consistent with what the curriculum is supposed to be and what the assessments are going to assess.
- the planned sequence of learning experiences the students are going through has continuity and a cumulative effect (Tyler 1949).

II. Instruction

A teacher carrying out this job well will make sure that the following tasks are accomplished:

- During instruction the students have to actively think about and use the ideas/skills being developed by talking about them with one another or using them in some other active way to solve a problem or answer a question (Applebee et al. 2003; Allington and Johnston 2001; Cazden 1992; Dillon 1988; Mehan 1979; Nystrand 1997). Thus, at appropriate points student thinking is made visible to the teacher and to other students through the design of the activities and interaction.

- The students know what the learning objective is and how the activity is supposed to help them learn or get better at it (Alexander, Frankiewicz, and Williams 1979; Lipsey and Wilson 1993; Waxman 1999; Wise and Okey 1983).

- The students see the relevance or importance of the intended learning (Marshall 1987).

- Students' current knowledge is activated and/or processing of new information is structured by Advance Organizers (Ausubel 1968; Lott 1983; Stone 1983).

- The students see the connection between what they're doing and their prior knowledge so the cognitive "Velcro" will more likely attach to the new material (Brewer and Treyens 1981; Hamaker 1986; Osman and Hannafin 1994; Pressley et al. 1990; Pressley et al. 1992).

- The students' understanding is checked frequently and broadly across all the students during instruction so they are not left behind while the teaching train rumbles on (Tobin and Capie 1982).

- Students experience an appropriate balance of higher-level questions despite the performance level of the class (i.e., no dumbing down of the thinking challenges even if academic skills are low) (Guzzetti et al. 1993; Redfield and Rousseau 1981; Wise and Okey 1983).

- The students experience a variety of learning experiences that allow for different learning styles.

- Design features from classical learning principles (e.g., Goal Setting; Practice; Contiguity) are built into student experiences where applicable to increase learning efficiency (See Saphier and Gower 1997, chapter on Principles of Learning.)

- Students are asked to identify similarities and differences between topics under study (Marzano et al. 2001).

- The students have to periodically summarize the meaning of the new learning at the end of instructional segments. [see six studies summarized in Marzano 2001. Average effect size 1.0 with average percentile gain of 34!] (Anderson and Hidi 1988/1989; Hattie et al. 1996; Rosenshine and Meister 1994).

- There are appropriate explanatory devices available to help students understand new and difficult skills and concepts. [like modeling thinking aloud; graphic organizers; imagery] (Aubusson et al. 1997; Griffin et al. 1992; Horton et al. 1990; Macklin 1997; McLaughlin 1991; Newton 1995; Pruitt 1993; Robinson and Kiewra 1996; Welch 1997; Willoughby et al. 1997).

- The students get frequent, detailed, corrective but non-judgmental feedback on their work. (Black and Wiliam 1998) [Effect sizes from .4 to .7 according to Marzano 2002] Bangert-Downs et al.1991; Hattie 1992; Lysakowski and Walberg 1981; Lysakowski and Walberg 1982; Scheerens and Bosker 1997; Trammel, Schloss and Alper 1994).

III. Motivation

A teacher carrying out this job well will make sure that the following tasks are accomplished:

- The students receive consistent messages in recurrent arenas of class life that their teachers believe in their ability to do quality work at high standards (Cotton 2001; Zimmerman and Blotner 1979).
- The students experience tenacity from their teachers in pressing them toward proficiency (Haberman 1995; Mitman and Lash 1988; Stipek and Daniels 1988).
- The students feel known and valued (Goldstein 1999; Noddings 1984; Tappan 1998; Sparks 2003; NRCIM 2003; Poplin and Weeres 1992; Resnick 1997; Combs 1982; McCombs and Whisler 1997).
- The students have regard and respect for their teacher (Lewis et al. 1996; Marzano and Pickering 2003b).
- The students perform engaging tasks that are thinking and problem-solving oriented and matched to their interests and developmental level.
- The students feel it is safe and supported to take intellectual risks and make mistakes (Haberman 1995).
- The students are taught to attribute success or failure to effort, not luck or task difficulty [average effect size .8 !] (Dweck 2000).
- The students get explicit instruction in how to exert effective effort (Ames 1987; VanOverwalle et al. 1989; Weinstein and Mayer 1986).
- The students know how to support and encourage one another to succeed (Schaps et al. in press; Bear 1998).
- The students have some ownership and choices in the rhythms of classroom life (Turner 1995; Emmer 1984; Emmer et al. 1981; Evertson et al. 2003; Doyle 1986) (Allington and Johnston 2001)

IV. Management

A teacher carrying out this job well will make sure that the following tasks are accomplished:

- The teacher's radar, body language and consequences are appropriately tuned to respond quickly and appropriately to off-task or disruptive behavior (Carr and Durand 1985; Emmer et al. 2003; Madsen et al. 1968).

- The students know exactly what the limits are, the rules mean, what the consequences are, and that they will be enforced consistently and without rancor (Jones 2000; Stage and Quiroz 1997; Brophy and Evertson 1976).

- The length of time segments at an activity and the kind of activity are a match for the students and the content.

- The arrangement of space supports the kind of student learning currently being done (Emmer 1984; Emmer et al. 1981; Evertson et al. 2003).

- The students experience no downtime, delay, confusion over directions, conflict over materials (Kounin 1970).

- The students receive an appropriate range of attention moves to maximize their engagement (Jones 2000; Stage and Quiroz 1997).

- The students know the routines and procedures of the room and can use them efficiently (Good and Brophy 2003; Evertson et al. 2003).

- Students are explicitly taught to work together and to self-manage in the fulfillment of academic tasks (Allington and Johnston 2001); (Taylor et al. 2000; Marzano et al. 2001).

The specific repertoire of ways to accomplish each of the tasks above is described elsewhere. (Saphier and Gower 1997 *The Skillful Teacher*.)

Each bullet above is only a "chapter heading" for each task of teaching. There dwells within each and every one of these 40 bullets a field of study in itself. For example, take the item "•Design features from classical learning principles are built into student experiences where applicable to increase learning efficiency." There are at least 24 separate little packages of power from classical learning theory to which this bullet refers, each of which is worth study on it's own, and each of which is known to increase the rate and durability of learning.

Some of the Principles of Learning are *small* and easily graspable, like "Close Confusers," which says to not introduce two ideas that are easily confusable in time proximity to one another. Introduce one and allow it to be solidly established through application before introducing the close confuser (like the letter "b" and "d". Another example: science text books often make the mistake of presenting "rotation" and "revolution" of the earth in the same page.)

Or the principle of "practice," which says practice a new skill in small units, and practice it frequently for short periods of time after first being introduced to it. Then space out practice sessions further and further apart. But continue to practice deliberately after attaining mastery ["overlearning,"] otherwise the "curve of forgetting" will catch you by surprise!

But other principles from classical learning theory are *big* and take time to learn and use properly, like "Goal Setting". This principle delineates a careful set of attributes and procedures for helping students learn to set goals that are clear, doable, and motivate one to fulfill them. Anyone interested in students' ownership of their own learning needs to know this technology.

Another quite different example: for the item "•The students receive consistent messages in recurrent arenas of class life that their teachers believe in their ability to do quality work at high standards." These messages are conveyed in a number of regularly recurring arenas where our language patterns send the messages. The arenas are such moments as when we:

- give students help,
- respond to student answers,
- convey assignments,
- deal with a student error.

Studying one's language patterns and the embedded messages in how we handle these everyday events is quite a subtle and significant area of teacher skill (*The Skillful Teacher* – Expectations chapter). Since it is tied to one's beliefs about students, it is not an area of study completed in a day!

Using the knowledge base outlined by the 40+ bullets is intellectually complicated, difficult, and demanding work. Acquiring professional knowledge takes considerable time and never quite ends, as is true for all real professions (e.g., medicine, engineering). Using this knowledge base well is required for teaching our children successfully, especially our poorest children who are academically behind. And it requires the conditions of a full profession to get our teachers able to do so.

Let us now turn to the final two areas of the professional knowledge base for teaching and learning.

V. Craft Knowledge for Teaching Specific Concepts and Skills – The Treasury of Subject-Specific Techniques for Making Learning Accessible to Students

Over two decades ago, Lee Shulman (1984) coined the term Pedagogical Content Knowledge. This term described the knowledge teachers have of how to teach their particular content. This meant content-specific repertoires of activities, examples, stories, equipment, readings, analogies that make the concepts and skills accessible to students. Such knowledge is craft knowledge. It is accumulated slowly over years of experience, of experimentation, of trading ideas with colleagues, and from good professional development. Like the other domains of professional knowledge we have profiled above, pedagogical content knowledge consists of repertoires, not right or best ways. The "Running Record" is a good tool for error analysis in primary students' oral reading, but it is not the only one. Knowing how to use that tool is a piece of pedagogical content knowledge. The important thing in reading instruction, however, is not that particular tool, but that a teacher have some way of carrying out the function that tool handles (i.e., consistently analyzing and recording students' proficiency at the skills of reading and using that data to plan that student's instruction). Here is another example of pedagogical content knowledge.

Students in the early grades of elementary school who have learned multiplication are used to an answer that is bigger than the numbers they multiplied together (15 x 15 = 225). Thus, it is confusing in higher grades when they learn that multiplication of fractions doesn't work that way. When you multiply fractions (1/3 x 1/2), the answer is *smaller* than either of the fractions you started with (1/3 x 1/2 = 1/6). How can this be?

A diagram using a rectangle can illustrate what 1/3 x 1/2 means and how the answer is a smaller fraction. The rectangle below represents a whole divided into halves.

If one takes 1/3 of the top half, one gets 1/6 of the whole rectangle.

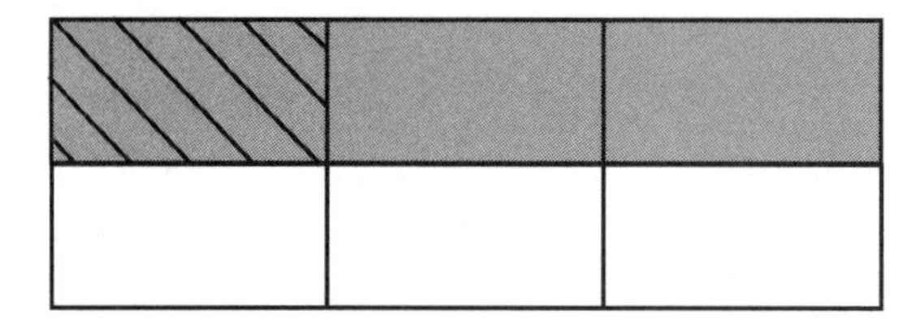

But "1/3 of" something doesn't feel like multiplication...it feels like you're dividing. So another way to illustrate the operation of multiplication of fractions is to overlay a drawing of 1/2 of the rectangle onto a drawing of 1/3 of the rectangle. The overlap turns out again to be 1/6.

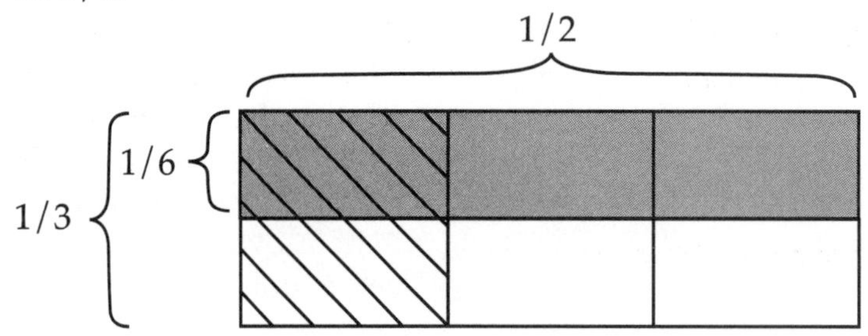

A teacher who knows how to use this rectangle model provides many students with the insight they need for understanding the counterintuitive way multiplication of fractions works. And that piece of teacher knowledge is an example of content-specific pedagogical knowledge.

Proficiency in this area of professional knowledge means:

- The teacher can use a fund of age-appropriate activities, materials, examples, analogies, comparisons, and readings to make accessible the concepts and skills of the discipline in multiple ways.

The text above describes pedagogical content knowledge at the micro level; that is, individual devices, examples, etc. that can make content clear and understandable for students. At the macro level, there also exists a repertoire of instructional approaches that are particular to academic subjects. Knowing different approaches and how to mix and match them to students is particularly apparent in teaching young students to read. Allington (2002) has demonstrated that it is teacher expertise that distinguishes successful reading instruction, not the use of any particular program or curriculum.

When teachers are well-versed in content-specific pedagogical knowledge at the macro level:

- students experience instruction that draws on different approaches in proper proportion to their individual learning needs. This form of expertise is particularly important in elementary literacy instruction but it is applicable at any level and in any subject (see Joyce and Weil, *Models of Teaching*).

Note: This section only has two "bullets". It is obvious, however, that if one drills down into any content-specific pedagogy, say 5th grade mathematics, with expert teachers of that content, one would have dozens of discrete "bullets" that should be available for everyone's repertoire – dozens of specific materials and examples that are powerful to use for, say, teaching the meaning of the equals sign ("="), which children commonly misunderstand to mean "perform an operation"...or "proportionality," which students typically never learn at all! The same is, of course, true for every content area at every grade level. No wonder commentators from John Dewey to the present have bemoaned the fact we have no way to pass on the "treasuries" of experienced teachers to the next generation![16]

VI. Understanding How the Ideas or Concepts in the Content are Connected – Hierarchical; Sequential; Parallel; Nested

There is another kind of knowledge related to the teaching of content that is different from the accumulated treasury of examples and instructional approaches we call pedagogical content knowledge. It is knowledge of how the concepts and skills one is teaching are con-

[16] "The successes of excellent teachers tend to be born and die with them: beneficial consequences extend only to those pupils who have personal contact with the gifted teachers. No one can measure the waste and loss that have come from the fact that the contributions of such men and women in the past have been thus confined." – The Sources of Science in Education, New York: Horace Liveright. 1929, p. 10.

nected to one another and how to bring these relationships to the attention of one's students. This includes an understanding of the network of concepts "that relate to the specific concept to be taught and of how that network is connected to the [content] in the yearlong curriculum as well as to the curricula of the previous and following years." (West and Staub 2003).

Mathematics is full of such networks, and understanding them profoundly effects a teacher's ability to teach for understanding. For example, Liping Ma (1999) points out that the concept of place value underlies the procedures for subtraction with regrouping and also the procedure for multi-digit multiplication. "The concept of place value, then, becomes a connection between these two topics."[p.119] – a connection that can influence and empower the teachers' teaching if the teacher understands the connection herself.

Teachers who understand these connections (be they sequence, hierarchy, parallel, or nested) don't keep them secret; they explicitly introduce them into their teaching. Stigler and Heibert found in the 1999 TIMMS video study that teachers from the highest performing nations in mathematics engaged students in the highest percentage of "rich mathematical problems that focus on *concepts and connections among mathematical ideas*." [italics not in original} (Stigler and Hiebert 2004).

This kind of knowledge about content is not assessed by teacher tests of content mastery typically used as a gateway for licensing. There is nothing wrong with such content tests, but they woefully underestimate the relationship between functional content mastery and the ability to teach that content to someone else. So for a well-developed teacher in this area it can be said that:

- The teacher knows the fundamental organizing ideas of the academic discipline—the "knowledge packages in the content" as Liping Ma says—and how they are connected to one another and intersect. These connections are an explicit part of a teacher's planning and are brought alive for the students.

- The teacher knows the prior knowledge hierarchy and sequence of learning that students typically need to master the content (e.g., see "21 Key Ideas about Fractions," Appendix D).

- The teacher knows the typical points of difficulty, confusion and also the misconceptions that are liable to arise in language, concepts, and interpretation.

The "21 Key Ideas about Fractions" at the end of this paper represent a concrete example for stimulating discussion about this kind of teacher knowledge—relationships of big ideas in the content.[17] The point of this example, however, is to illustrate that there exists in *every* content area this same kind of knowledge about big ideas and their relationships. Understanding how to surface these relationships is essential for teachers to know explicitly and incorporate in their planning.

[17] I believe that high school algebra teachers may also find some useful insights here into problems their students are having due to failure to learn these big ideas in elementary school. As some of our readers will surely testify, an elementary student can pass fraction tests all the way through the grades by memorizing algorithms, but run into trouble in algebra because he/she didn't really understand the fundamental concepts of fractions.

Appendix B: High Functioning Teams

The Engine of Improvement in Schools That Gets Big Learning Gains for Their Students Is High Functioning Teams

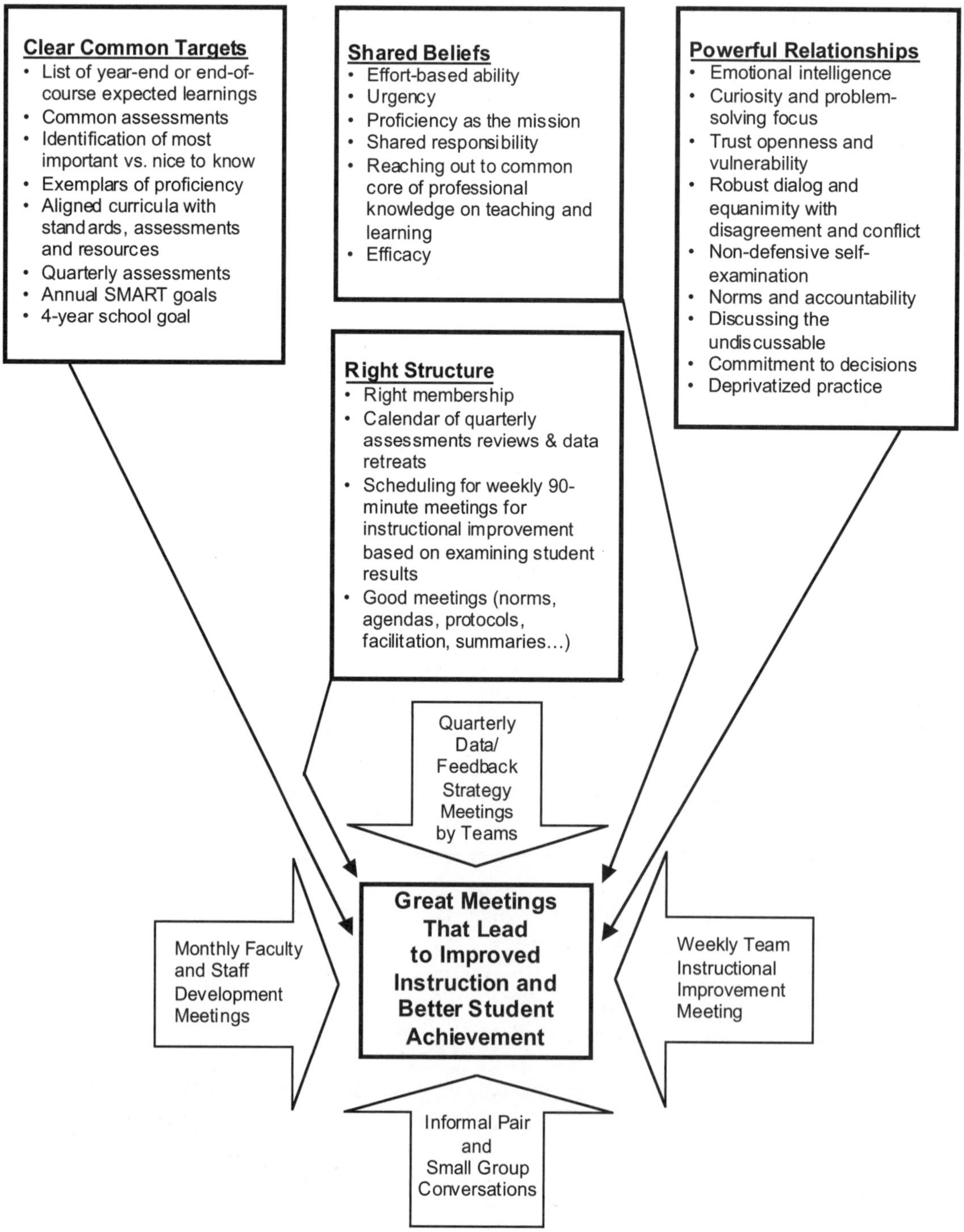

Clear Common Targets
- List of year-end or end-of-course expected learnings
- Common assessments
- Identification of most important vs. nice to know
- Exemplars of proficiency
- Aligned curricula with standards, assessments and resources
- Quarterly assessments
- Annual SMART goals
- 4-year school goal

Shared Beliefs
- Effort-based ability
- Urgency
- Proficiency as the mission
- Shared responsibility
- Reaching out to common core of professional knowledge on teaching and learning
- Efficacy

Powerful Relationships
- Emotional intelligence
- Curiosity and problem-solving focus
- Trust openness and vulnerability
- Robust dialog and equanimity with disagreement and conflict
- Non-defensive self-examination
- Norms and accountability
- Discussing the undiscussable
- Commitment to decisions
- Deprivatized practice

Right Structure
- Right membership
- Calendar of quarterly assessments reviews & data retreats
- Scheduling for weekly 90-minute meetings for instructional improvement based on examining student results
- Good meetings (norms, agendas, protocols, facilitation, summaries...)

Quarterly Data/ Feedback Strategy Meetings by Teams

Monthly Faculty and Staff Development Meetings

Great Meetings That Lead to Improved Instruction and Better Student Achievement

Weekly Team Instructional Improvement Meeting

Informal Pair and Small Group Conversations

Appendix C: On Becoming a Profession

A profession has certain recognizable attributes. Though thousands of individuals who teach act in a highly professional manner, teaching is not now a profession.

Professions have:

- an acknowledged knowledge base, the nature of which is Areas of Performance, Repertoire, Matching (*all* true professional knowledge is so constituted).
- rigorous training and certification of members
- systematic enculturation of new members
- required and continuous learning regularly built-in to the work cycle
- culture of high consulting and collaboration
- high public accountability
- internal maintenance of high standards of practice
- consider themselves able to influence and responsible for client results
- members who make autonomous decisions guided by a canon of ethics

In a profession, leadership comes from a practitioner who is seen as the head practitioner: the Medical Director in a hospital; the Senior Partner in a law firm or an architecture firm. The "practice" (firm/hospital/HMO) hires an administrator for the business end. The Head Practitioner is the true leader of the organization.

> Doctors are not scientists, at least not in their medical roles, because though they certainly draw on science, what they do is neither objective enough nor oriented to the production of new knowledge — nor should it be. And they are certainly not artists, since aesthetic principles and independent creativity have little or no place in practice, despite everything that has been said about the 'art' of medicine. But doctors are craftspeople of the highest order. Sometimes, like engineers, they lean very heavily on science. Sometimes, like diamond cutters, they seem to be coasting along on pure skill. And occasionally, like glassblowers or goldsmiths, what they do verges on art.
>
> – Mel Konner, *Becoming a Doctor*,
> Elisabeth Sifton Books/Viking, New York: 1987.

Committing to expert teaching based on knowledge is the foundation of professionalization. The focus on poor children is the social agenda based on the growing inequality in the country and the need to fulfill the promise of democracy, and equally on the economic need for an educated competitive workforce for a 21st century economy.

Appendix D: 21 Key Ideas About Fractions

The following understandings are examples of the sixth kind of expertise in the common core of professional knowledge – Understanding How the Ideas or Concepts in the Content are Connected—Hierarchical; Sequential; Parallel; Nested . They are listed, roughly, in order of cumulative and increasing complexity. They are not written necessarily in kid language; but they do lay out the sequence of understandings kids need in order to master operations with fractions reliably. Failure to understand these big ideas forecloses success in algebra later on, even if youngsters fool us for a while by memorizing algorithms and developing work-around strategies.

1. Fractional parts are equal shares or equal-sized portions of a whole thing or a whole set.

2. There are five ways of representing fractions or five visual models of what fractional parts mean: taking a fraction (1) of an area, (2) of a line, (3) of a set, and (4) of a three-dimensional object (volume). (A fifth way is as a ratio of sets. This comes later in the sequence).

3. Fractional parts have special names (e.g., thirds, fourths, fifths...) that tell how many equal parts of that size are needed to make a whole. (three thirds, four fourths, five fifths...)

4. The more equal parts required to make a whole, the smaller the parts. So for a given whole, a higher number of parts (8/8ths vs 3/3rds) means each piece is a smaller size share.

5. The denominator (bottom part of the fraction) tells us how many equal parts into which the whole was divided. The numerator (top part of the fraction) tells us how many of those parts we've got (how many parts are being considered).

6. Fractions can be part of a set of discrete objects (a half dozen eggs... 3/4 of the number of the children in the class). In this kind of case, the denomimator refers to the number of equal sized groups into which the set is divided, and the numerator refers to the number of groups currently under consideration.

7. When you increase the numerator of a fraction and keep the denominator the same, you have more of the same size piece and thus a greater area / amount / quantity / volume overall.

8. When you keep the numerator the same and increase the denominator, you have the same number of pieces, but the pieces are smaller, and thus you have less of the whole thing / set / length / volume overall.

9. The equal shares that make up fractions don't have to be congruent (don't have to be identical in shape) but they must be equal in total area / number / length / volume (for the four cases.)

10. Fractions can represent an area / amount / length / volume larger than a whole.

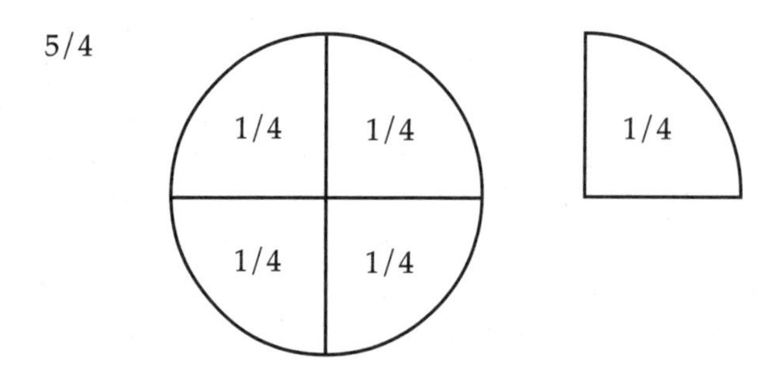

11. Two equivalent fractions (2/3 = 4/6) are two ways of describing the same amount / length / area / volume / relationship. It's just that you're using different size portions to add up to the same total amount. In fact, each fraction has not just two but an infinite number of symbolic (same value) representations; e.g., 1/2 =2/4=3/6=4/8=5/10...

12. In fractions, you need to be talking about the same whole in order to compare two or more fractions. For example, when talking about 1/2 of the object (or set or line we're referring to), the size of the whole is the determining factor in how big 1/2 is. Suppose we want to say that 1/2 = 2/4; the 1/2 is half of something real (an object, a set). It's equal to 2/4 of that particular thing or set, and not equal to 2/4 of a different thing that's not the same size. When we're talking about equivalent fractions, 1/2 is only equal to 2/4, if we're talking about the same whole or wholes of the same size.

13. When you're talking about fractions, you're always talking about a relationship.

14. The whole doesn't have to be a "whole," as the following example illustrates.

    The label of a fractional piece of the whole is determined by the whole that is the starting point of the problem. For example, consider the following: "There was 3/4 of a gallon of ice cream in the freezer. (The whole that is the starting point is a *whole gallon of ice cream*, of which we now have 3/4. So 3/4 of a gallon becomes the new whole.) One day Paula came in with some friends and ate 2/3 of the ice cream in the freezer. [That means: divide the ice cream you have at the start (3/4 gallon) into three parts (three quarters) and take two of them away 'cause Paula ate them (two quarters)]. How much ice cream is now left in the freezer?" Answer: 1/4 of a gallon.

    If we use manipulatives or draw a diagram and set out 3/4 of a gallon, each of those three one-quarter sized pieces will be 1/4 of a gallon of ice cream.

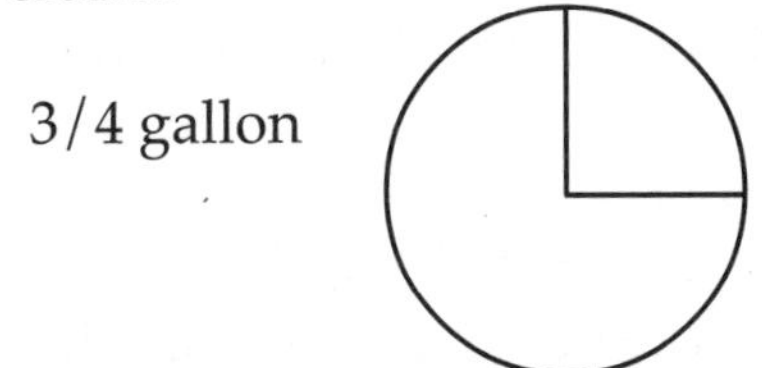

    If we are figuring out the amount of this that was eaten that day, that is, 2/3 of the ice cream, that would be 2/3 of the 3/4, or two of the three parts that are in the freezer.

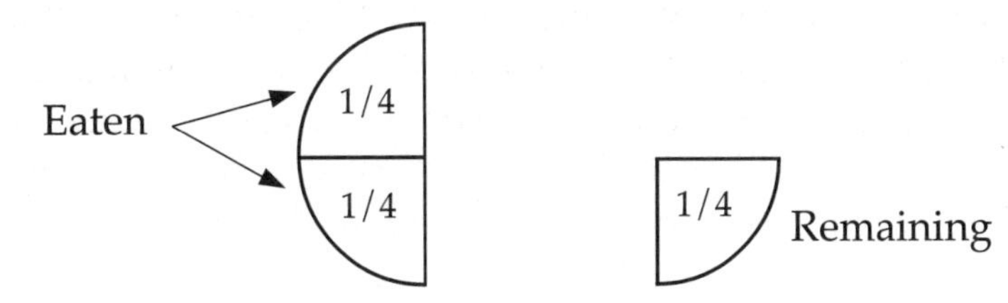

Since each of these parts was worth 1/4 and two of them are gone, that leaves 1/4 remaining = 1/4 of a gallon of ice cream. When we look at the single piece that is left, we see that it is 1/4 of the gallon that was first brought home, even though it's 1/3 of the amount of ice cream Paula and the Greedies found when they first came in. The hard part is to remember that the whole we are always working in reference to is the original gallon. Wow!

15. When we line up a set of fractions in order, from smallest to largest, we can use benchmarks to determine their relative value to each other; for example, determining which fractions mean more than 1/2 and which mean less. Or we may ask ourselves about how close to zero a fraction is as opposed to how close to one.

16. Common fraction notation and decimal fraction notation are alternative ways of naming the same rational number. Decimal fractions are all fractions with ten or a power of ten as the denomimator. Percentages are the same as decimal numbers to two places. The "whole" in percentages is always 100. The % sign at the end replaces the decimal point at the beginning. Common fractions, as opposed to decimals and percentages, can have any denominator (except zero).

17. Fractional notation can be another way of saying "divide two numbers. Find out how many of the bottom one (denominator) can fit into the top one (numerator)."

18. You can also divide two numbers where the one going in to the others is actually bigger! "3 divided by 5"...meaning if you divide 3 into 5 equal sized portions, how big will each be? (You have three big cookies and you want to give equal amounts of cookie to five people. How much would each person get?)

19. Fractions can express the ratio between two quantities (For every 3 girls there are 5 boys.)

20. Fractions can be operators (an instruction to operate) (i.e., a number that operates on another number in the sense of stretching or shrinking the magnitude of the number [a doll house is 1/12 the size of a real house. How big is the real house]).

21. The preferred way of representing a fraction is with the smallest possible denominator you can; you can get this by getting the numerator and denominator so they have no common factors.

Thanks to Ellen Davidson, Lucy West, and the math coaches of NYC's District 2 for their critique and input on the 21 ideas above.

The approach of identifying Big Ideas in the teaching of mathematics is an organizing concept in John Van de Walle's book, *Elementary and Middle School Mathematics – Teaching Developmentally*. We have taken this approach and gone into depth with it for fractions only. Thanks to Dr. Van de Walle for his insight into the utility of this organizing principal for developing teachers' pedagogical knowledge.

Bibliography

Alexander, L., R. Frankiewicz, and R. Williams. "Facilitation of Learning and Retention of Oral Instruction Using Advance Post organizers." *Journal of Educational* Psychology 71, 7-1707 (1979).

Alexander, Patricia, Ed. *Educational Psychologist* (Spring 1996).

Allington, Richard L. "You Can't Learn Much From Books You Can't Read." *Educational Leadership* 60 (November 2002): 16-19.

Allington, Richard L., and Peter H. Johnston. "What Do We Know About Effective Fourth-Grade Teachers and Their Classrooms?" In Cathy M. Roller (Ed.), *Learning to Teach.* Newark: International Reading Association, 2001.

American Gaming Association, 2003. www.americangaming.org/Industry/factsheets/statistics_detail.cfv?id=7.

Ames, C. "The Enhancement of Student Motivation." In M. Maehr and D. Kleiber (Eds.), *Advances in Motivation and Achievement . Vol. 5: Enhancing Motivation.* Greenwich, CT: JAI Press, 1987.

Anderson, V., and S. Hidi. "Teaching Students to Summarize." *Educational Leadership* 46 (1988/1989): 26-28.

Applebee, Arthur N., Judith A. Langer, Martin Nystrand, and Adam Gamoran. "Discussion-Based Approaches to Developing Understanding: Classroom Instruction and Student Performance in Middle and High School English." *American Educational Research Journal* 40 (Fall 2003): 685-730.

Aubusson, P., S. Foswill, R. Barr, and L. Perkovic. "What Happens When Students Do Simulation-Role-Play in Science." *Research in Science Education* 27(4) (1997): 565-579.

Ausubel, D. P. *Educational Psychology: A Cognitive View.* New York: Holt, Rinehart and Winston, 1968.

Bangert-Downs, R. L., C. C. Kulik, J. A. Kulick, and M. Morgan. "The Instructional Effects of Feedback in Test-Like Events." *Review of Educational Research* 61(2) (1991): 213-238.

Barth, Roland, "The Culture Builder." *Educational Leadership*, May 2002.

Battistich, V., M. Watson, D. Solomon, E. Schaps, and J. Solomon. "The Child Development Project: A Comprehensive Program for the Development of Prosocial Character." In W. M. Kurtines and J. L. Gerwitz (Eds.), *Handbook of Moral Behavior and Development: Vol. 3 Application* (pp.1-34). Hillsdale: Erlbaum, 1991.

Bear, G. G. "School Discipline in the United States: Prevention, Control, and Long-Term Social Development." *School Psychology Review* 27(1)(1998), 14-32.

Bellah, Robert N. *Habits of the Heart: Individualism and Commitment in American Life.* Berkeley, University of California Press, 1996.

Bereiter, C. and M. Scardamalia. *Surpassing Ourselves: an Inquiry into the Nature of Implications of Expertise.* Chicago: Open Court, 1993, 153-181.

Black, Paul, and Dylan Wiliam. "Inside the Black Box: Raising Standards Through Classroom Assessment." *Phi Delta Kappan* (October 1998): 139-148.

Bloom, B.S. *Learning for Mastery.* Evaluation Comment. UCLA-CSEIP, I, h.p.

Brewer, W. F., and J. C. Treyens. "Role of Schemata in Memory for Places." *Cognitive Psychology* 13 (1981): 207-230.

Brophy, J. E., and C. M. Evertson. *Learning From Teaching: A Developmental Perspective.* Boston: Allyn & Bacon, 1976.

Camilli, Gregory and Paula Wolfe. "Research on Reading: A Cautionary Tale." *Educational Leadership* (March 2004): 26-29.

Carr, E. G., and V. M. Durand. "Reducing Behavior Problems Through Functional Communication Training." *Journal of Applied Behavior Analysis* 18 (1985): 111-126.

Carroll, J.B. " A Model for School Learning." *Teachers College Record,64 (8)*, 723-733.

Carroll, Tom, Kathleen Fulton, Karen Abercrombie, and Irene Yoon. "Fifty Years After Brown v. Board of Education: a Two-Tiered Education System." Prepared for the National Commission on Teaching and America's Future, Washington, DC, May 13, 2004.

Cazden, C. B. "Revealing and Telling: The Socialization of Attention in Learning to Read and Write." *Educational Psychology,* 12 (1992):305-313.

Charles A. Dana Center. *Hope for Urban Education: A Study of Nine High-Performing, High-Poverty, Urban Elementary Schools.* The Charles A. Dana Center: University of Texas / Austin for the US Dept. of Education, 1999.

Combs, A. W. *A Personal Approach to Teaching; Beliefs That Make a Difference.* Boston: Allyn & Bacon, 1982.

Comer, James P. and Michael Ben-Avie. *Child by Child: The Comer Process for Change in Education.* New York City: Teachers' College Press, 1999.

Comer, James P. , Norris M. Haynes, Edward T. Joyner, and Michael Ben-Avie. *Rallying the Whole Village: The Comer Process for Reforming Education.* New York City: Teachers' College Press, 1996.

Cotton, Kathleen. "Expectations and Student Outcomes". School Improvement Research Series. Northwest Regional Educational Laboratory. Portland, OR: 2001.

Daggett, Willard. "21st Century Literacy – The Challenge to Schools". International Center for Leadership in Education. Rexford, NY: 2002.

Darling-Hammond, Linda. In *What Matters Most: Teaching for America's Future.* The National Commission on Teaching & America's Future. Woodbridge, VA: 1996.

D'Auria, John. "Factors That Influence How Children Come To Perceive Their Intelligence As A Dynamic Quality." Dissertation University of Massachusetts, 2001.

DePree, Max. *Leading Without Power: Finding Hope in Serving Community.* San Francisco: Jossey-Bass, 1997.

Dillon, J. T. "The Remedial Status of Student Questioning." *Curriculum Studies* 20 (1988): 197-210.

Doyle, W. "Classroom Organization and Management." In M. C. Wittrock (Ed.), *Handbook of Research on Teaching* (3rd. ed., pp. 392-431). New York: Macmillan, 1986.

DuFour, Richard, Rebecca DuFour, Robert Eaker, and Gayle Karhanek. *Whatever It Takes: How Professional Learning Communities Respond When Kids Don't Learn*. Bloomington: National Education Service, 2004.

DuFour, Richard, Robert Eaker, and Rebecca DuFour. *On Common Ground: The Power of Professional Learning Communities*. Bloomington: National Education Service, 2005.

DuFour, Richard and Robert Eaker. *Professional Learning Communities at Work: Best Practices for Enhancing Student Achievement.* Alexandria: ASCD, 1998.

Dunkin, Michael J. and Bruce J. Biddle. *The Study of Teaching.* New York: Holt, Rinehart and Winston, Inc., 1974.

Dweck, Carol S. *Self-Theories: Their Role in Motivation, Personality and Development (Essays in Social Psychology).* Psychology Press, 2000.

Eaton, J.F., C.W. Anderson and E.L.Smith. "Students' Misconceptions Interfere with Science Learning: Case Studies of Fifth Grade Students." *Elementary School Journal* 84, no. 4 (1984): 32-41.

Eylon, B., and M.C.Linn, "Learning and Instruction: An Examination of Four ResearchPerspectives in Science Education." *Review of Educational Research* 58, no.3 (1988).

Edmonds, R.R. and J.R. Frederiksen. *Search for Effective Schools: The Identification and Analysis of City Schools That Are Instructionally Effective for Poor Children.* Cambridge, MA: Harvard University Center for Urban Studies, 1978.

Elmore, Richard. "Leadership for Large-Scale Improvement in American Education." Unpublished paper, September 1999.

Elmore, Richard, and Deanna Burney. "Staff Development and Instructional Improvement, Community District 2, New York City." New York: National Commission on Teaching and America's Future (March 1996).

Emmer, E. T. *Classroom Management: Research and Implications.* ERIC Report ED251448. Austin, TX: Research and Development Center for Teacher Education, University of Texas, 1984.

Emmer, E. T., C. M. Evertson, and M. E. Worsham. *Classroom Management for Secondary Teachers* (6th ed.). Boston: Allyn & Bacon, 2003.

Emmer, E. T., J. P. Sanford, C. M. Evertson, B. S. Clements, and J. Martin. *The Classroom Management Improvement Study: An Experiment in Elementary School Classrooms.* R & D Report No. 6050. Austin, TX: Research and Development Center for Teacher Education, University of Texas, 1981 (ERIC Report ED226452).

Evertson, C. M., E. T. Emmer, and M. E. Worsham. *Classroom Management for Elementary Teachers* (6th ed.). Boston: Allyn and Bacon, 2003.

Federal Reserve Bank of Minneapolis. *Fedgazette.* March 2003. http://minneapolisfed.org/pubs/fedgaz/03-03/expend.cfm

Feiman-Nemser, Sharon. "From Preparation to Practice: Designing a Continuum to Strengthen and Sustain Teaching." Teachers College Record 103/6, Dec. 2001.

Feiman-Nemser, Sharon. "What New Teachers Need to Learn". *Educational Leadership* (May 2003).

Frederiksen, J.R. and B. Y. White. "Reflective Assessment of Students' Research Within an Inquiry-Based Middle School Science Curriculum." Paper presented at the annual meeting of the American Educational Association, Chicago, March 1997.

Fullan, Michael with Suzanne Stiegelbauer. *The New Meaning of Educational Change.* 2nd ed. New York: Teachers College Press, 1991.

Goldstein, L. S. "The Relational Zone: The Role of Caring Relationships in the Co-Construction of Mind." *American Educational Research Journal* 36 (3): 647-673.

Goleman, Daniel. *Emotional Intelligence: Why it Can Matter More Than IQ.* New York: Bantam, 1999.

Good, T. L., and J. E. Brophy. *Looking in Classrooms* (9th ed.). Boston: Allyn & Bacon, 2003.

Gould, Stephen Jay. *The Mismeasure of Man.* New York: W.W. Norton & Co.: 1981 and 1996.

Griffin, C., D. C. Simmons, and E. J. Kameenui. "Investigating the Effectiveness of Graphic Organizer Instruction on the Comprehension and Recall of Science Content by Students with Learning Disabilities." *Journal of Reading, Writing & Learning Disabilities International* 7(4) (1992): 355-376.

Gross, S. *Final Report, Mathematics Content/Connections Elementary Science in Montgomery County (Maryland): A Comprehensive Transformation of a System-Wide Science Program.* Rockville: Montgomery County Public Schools, July 1999.

Grossman, Kate N., Becky Beaupre, and Rosiland Rossi. "Poorest Kids Often Wind up with the Weakest Teachers." *Chicago Sun-Times Failing Teachers Series* Feb. 6, 2002: 13-32.

Guzzetti, B. J., T. E. Snyder, and G. V. Glass. "Promoting Conceptual Change in Science: A Comparative Meta-Analysis of Instructional Interventions From Reading Education and Science Education." *Reading Research Quarterly* 28(2) (1993): 117-155.

Haberman, M. "Selecting 'Star' Teachers for Children and Youth in Urban Poverty." *Phi Delta Kappan* 76(10) (1995): 777-781.

Hamaker, C. "The Effects of Adjunct Questions on Prose Learning." *Review of Educational Research* 56 (1986):212-242.

Hancock vs. Driscoll and the Commonwealth of Massachusetts, April 2004.

Hattie, J. A. "Measuring the Effects of Schooling." *Australian Journal of Education* 3691: (1992): 5-13.

Hattie, J., J. Biggs, and N. Purdi. "Effects of Learning Skills Interventions on Student Learning: A Meta-Analysis." *Review of Educational Research* 66(2) (1996): 99-136.

Haycock, Kati. *A Dream Deferred.* Washington, D.C.: Education Trust, 2004.

Heibert, James, Ronald Gallimore, and James Stigler. "A Knowledge Base for the Teaching Profession: What Would it Look Like and How Can We Get One." *Educaional Researcher,* Vol. 31, Number 5, June/July 2002.

Heifetz, Ronald A., and Donald L. Laurie. "The Work of Leadership". *Harvard Business Review* (Feb. 2000).

Hershberg, Theodore. "The Case for New Standards in Education." *Education Week* (Dec. 10, 1997).

Horton, S. V., T. C. Lovitt, and D. Bergerud. "The Effectiveness of Graphic Organizers for Three Classifications of Secondary Students in Content Area Classes." *Journal of Learning Disabilities* 23(1) (1990): 12-22.

Howard, Jeff. "Getting Smart: The Social Construction of Intelligence." Lexington, MA, The Efficacy Institute, Inc., 1990.

Jackson, D. Bruce. "Education Reform as if Student Agency Mattered: Academic Microcultures and Student Identity." *Phi Delta Kappan* (84) 8 (April 2003): 579-591.

Jencks, Christopher. "Our Unequal Democracy: Economic and Political Inequality Reinforce Each Other and Compromise Democracy." *The American Prospect* 15(6) 9 June 2004.

Jerald, Craig D. *Dispelling the Myth Revisited: Preliminary Findings from a Nationwide Analysis of "High-Flying" Schools.* The Education Trust, 2001.

Jones, Fred. *Tools For Teaching: Discipline, Instruction, Motivation.* Santa Cruz: Frederic Jones & Associates, 2000.

Joyce, Bruce, Marsha Weil, and Emily Calhoun. *Models of Teaching.* Boston: Allyn & Bacon, 1999.

Kounin, J. S. *Discipline and Group Management in Classrooms.* New York: Holt, Rinehart & Winston, 1970.

Laczko-Kerr, I., and D. Berliner. "In Harm's Way: How Undercertified Teachers Hurt Their Students." *Educational Leadership* (May 2003): 34-38.

Ladson-Billings, G. *The Dreamkeepers: Successful Teachers of African-American Children.* San Francisco: Jossey-Bass, 1994.

Langer, Judith A. "Excellence in English in Middle and High School: How Teachers' Professional Lives Support Student Achievement." *American Educational Research Journal* 37, no. 2 (Summer 2000): 397-439.

Lewis, C., E. Schapps, and M. Watson. "The Caring Classroom's Academic Edge." *Educational Leadership*, 54(1), 16-21.

Lipsey, M. W., and D. B. Wilson. "The Efficacy of Psychological, Educational, and Behavioral Treatment." *American Psychologist* 48(12) 1993): 1181-1209.

Little, J. W. "Norms of Collegiality and Experimentation: Workplace Conditions of School Success." *American Educational Research Journal* (Fall 1982).

Little, Judith Warren. "The Persistence of Privacy: Autonomy and Initiative in Teachers' Professional Relations." *Teachers College Record* 91 (1990): 509-536.

Lott, G. W. "The Effect of Inquiry Teaching and Advanced Organizers Upon Student Outcomes in Science Education." *Journal of Research in Science Teaching* 20(5) (1983): 437-451.

Louis, Karen Seashore, and Sharon D. Kruse. *Professionalism and Community.* Thousand Oaks: Corwin Press, 1995.

Lysakowski, R. S., and H. J. Walberg. "Classroom Reinforcement in Relation to Learning: A Quantitative Analysis." *Journal of Educational Research* 75 (1981): 69-77.

Lysakowski, R. S., and H. J. Walberg. "Instructional Effects of Cues, Participation, and Corrective Feedback: A Quantitative Synthesis. "*American Educational Research Journal* 19(4) (1982): 559-578.

Ma, Liping. *Knowing and Teaching Elementary Mathematics: Teachers' Understanding of Fundamental Mathematics in China and the United States.* Mahwah: Lea Publishers, 1999.

Macklin, M. C. "Preschoolers' Learning of Brand Names For Visual Cues." *Journal of Consumer Research* 23(3) (1997): 251-261.

Madsen, C. H., Jr., W. C. Becker, and D. R. Thomas. "Rules, Praise, and Ignoring: Elements or Elementary Classroom Control." *Journal of Applied Behavior Analysis* 1, (1968): 139-150.

Marshall, H. "Motivational Strategies of Three Fifth-Grade Teachers." *Elementary School Journal* 88, (1987): 135-150.

Marzano, Robert J., Debra J.Pickering, and Jane E. Pollock. *Classroom Instruction That Works.* Alexandria: ASCD, 2001.

Marzano, R. J., (with J. S. Marzano and D. J. Pickering). *Classroom Management That Works.* Alexandria: ASCD, 2003b.

McCombs, B. L., and J. S. Whisler. *The Learner-Centered Classroom and School.* San Francisco: Jossey-Bass, 1997.

McLaughlin, E. M. "Effects of Graphic Organizers and Levels of Text Difficulty on Less-Proficient Fifth-Grade Reader's Comprehension of Expository Text." *Dissertation Abstracts International* Vol. 51(9-A) (1991): 3028.

Mehan, H. *Learning Lessons: Social Organization in the Classroom.* Cambridge: Harvard University Press, 1979.

Mendro, Robert L. "Student Achievement and School and Teacher Accountability." *Journal of Personnel Evaluation in Education* 12(3) (1998).

Mendro, Robert, and Karen Bebry. "School Evaluation: A Change in Perspective." Paper presented at the Annual Meeting of the AERA, New Orleans, April 24-28, 2000.

Milanowski, Anthony. Educational Policy Archives, Vol. 11, no.50 (Dec. 27, 2003). Retrieved from http://epaa.asu.edu/epaa/v11n50/

Milken, Lowell. *A Matter of Quality: A Strategy for Assuring the High Quality of America's Teachers*. Milken Family Foundation: Santa Monica, CA, 1999.

Miller, Matthew. "Teaching Poor Students: How to Make it a Prestigious Desirable Career." *American Educator* 27, No. 4 (winter 2003/2004): 28-37.

Minkoff, Maxine. *Head of the Class: Characteristics of Higher Performing Urban High Schools in Massachusetts*. Boston: Center for Education Research and Policy at Mass INC, 2003.

Mitman, A. and A. Lash. "Students' Perception of Their Academic Standing and Classroom Behavior." *Elementary School Journal 89 (1988): 55-68.*

Mortimer, P., P. P. Sammons, L. Stoll, D. Lewis, and R. Ecob. *School Matters*. Somerset Wells: Open Books, 1988.

Muijis, R., and D. Reynolds. "Effective Mathematics Teaching: Year 2 of a Research Project." Paper presented at the International Conference on School Effectiveness and School Improvement. Hong Kong, August 2000.

Murnane, Richard J. and Frank Levy. *Teaching the New Basic Skills: Principles for Educating Children to Thrive in a Changing Economy.* New York: Martin Kessler Books/The Free Press, 1996.

National Alliance of Business. "Investing in Teaching." Washington, D.C., 2001.

National Alliance of Business. "Investing in Teaching: Databook." Washington, D.C., 2001.

National Association of Secondary School Principals (NASSP). *Breakthrough High Schools: You Can Do It, Too! Volume 1*. Reston, VA, 2004.

National Association of State Boards of Education. "The Numbers Game: Ensuring Quantity and Quality in the Teaching Work Force." Alexandria, VA, 1998.

National Center for Education Statistics. "Elementary and Secondary Education: An International Perspective". Office of Educational Research and Improvement, U.S. Dept. of Education, 2000.

National Center for Education Statistics. "Outcomes of Learning: Results from the 2000 Program for International Student Assessment of 15-Year-Olds in Reading, Mathematics and Science Literacy". Office of Educational Research and Improvement, U.S. Dept. of Education, December 2001.

National Research Council Institute of Medicine. *Engaging Schools: Fostering High School Students' Engagement and Motivation to Learn.* Washington, D.C.: National Academies Press, 2003.

Newmann, F., and Gary G. Wehlage. *Successful School Restructuring.* Madison, Wisconsin: Center on Organization and Restructuring of Schools, 1995.

Newton, D. P. "Pictorial Support for Discourse Comprehension." *British Journal of Educational Psychology* 64(2) (1995): 221-229.

Noddings, N. *Caring: A Feminine Approach to Ethics and Moral Education.* Berkeley: University of California Press, 1984.

Nystrand, M., A. Gamoran, R. Kachur, and C. Prednergast. *Opening Dialogue: Understanding the Dynamics of Language and Learning in the English Classroom.* New York: Teachers College Press, 1997.

Osman, M., and M. J. Hannafin. "Effects of Advance Organizing Questioning and Prior Knowledge on Science Learning." *Journal of Educational Research* 88(1) (1994): 5-13.

Perkins, David. *Outsmarting IQ: The Emerging Science of Learnable Intelligence.* New York: Free Press, 1995.

Perry, Theresa, Claude Steele, and Asa Hilliard. *Young, Gifted and Black: Promoting High Achievement Among African-American Students.* Boston: Beacon, 2003.

Phillips, Kevin. *Wealth and Democracy: A Political History of the American Rich.* New York: Broadway Books, 2002.

Poplin, Mary, and Joseph Weeres. *Voices From the Inside: a Report on Schooling from Inside the Classroom.* Claremont: The Institute for Education Transformation (Claremont Graduate School),1992.

Pressley, Michael, et al. "The Nature of Effective First-Grade Literacy Instruction." 1998.

Pressley, M., R. Tenenbaum, M. McDaniel, and E. Wood. "What Happens When University Students Try to Answer Prequestions That Accompany Textbook Material?" *Contemporary Educational Psychology* 15 (1990): 27-35.

Pressley, M., E. Wood, V. Woloshyn, V. Martin, A. King, and D. Menke. "Encouraging Mindful Use of Prior Knowledge: Attempting to Construct Explanatory Answers Facilitates Learning." *Educational Psychologist* 27(1) (1992): 91-109.

Pruitt, N. *Using Graphics in Content Area Subjects.* Master's thesis, Kean College of New Jersey. ERIC Document No. ED355483. 1993.

Redfield, D. L., and E. W. Rousseau. "A Meta-Analysis of Experimental Research on Teacher Questioning Behavior." *Review of Educational Research* 51(2) (1981): 237-245.

Reeves, Douglas B. *The Leader's Guide to Standards; A Blueprint for Educational Equity and Excellence.* San Francisco: Jossey-Bass, 2002.

Resnick, M., et al. "Protecting Adolescents From Harm: Findings From the National Longitudinal Study on Adolescents' Health." *Journal of the American Medical Association,* 278 (1997): 823-832.

Robinson, D. H., and K. A. Kiewra. "Visual Argument: Graphic Organizers Are Superior to Outlines in Improving Learning From Text." *Journal of Educational Psychology* 87(3) (1996): 455-467.

Rosenshine, B., and C. C. Meister. "Reciprocal Teaching: A Review of the Research." *Review of Educational Research* 64(4) (1994): 479-530.

Rothstein, Richard. *Class and Schools: Using Social, Economic and Educational Reform to Close the Black-White Achievement Gap.* Washington: Economic Policy Institute, 2004.

Sanders, W. L., and J. C. Rivers. "Cumulative and Residual Effects of Teachers on Future Academic Achievement." Knoxville: University of Tennessee Value-Added Research and Assessment Center, 1996.

Saphier, J. D., and R. Gower. *The Skillful Teacher.* Acton: Research for Better Teaching, 1997.

Saphier, J. D. *How to Make Supervision and Evaluation Really Work.* Carlisle: Research for Better Teaching, 1993.

Saphier, J. D., and M. King. "Good Seeds Grow in Strong Cultures." *Educational Leadership* (March 1985).

Schaps, E., V. Battistich, and D. Solomon. "Community in School As Key to Student Growth: Findings From the Child Development Project." In R. Weissberg, J. Zins, and H. Walberg (Eds.), *Building School Success on Social and Emotional Learning*. New York: Teachers College Press, in press.

Scheerens, J., and R. Bosker. *The Foundations of Educational Effectiveness.* New York: Pergamon, 1997.

Schlechty, Phillip C. *Shaking Up the Schoolhouse: How to Support and Sustain Educational Innovation*. San Francisco: Jossey-Bass, 2001.

Sherman, Joel D., Steven D. Honegger, and Jennifer L. McGivern. "Comparative Indicators of Education in the United States and Other G8 Countries: 2002". National Center for Education Statistics. Office of Educational Research and Improvement, U.S. Dept. of Education, May 2003.

Shulman, Lee. "Paradigms and Research Programs in the Study of Teaching: A Contemporary Perspective." In Merlin C. Wittrock (Ed.) *Handbook of Research on Teaching* (3rd ed.). New York: Macmillan, 1986.

Sparks, Dennis. "We Care, Therefore They Learn." *Journal of Staff Development*, 24(4) (Fall 2003): 42-47.

Stage, S. A., and D. R. Quiroz. " A Meta-Analysis of Interventions to Decrease Disruptive Classroom Behavior in Public Education Settings." *School Psychology Review* 26(3) (1977): 333-368.

Starr, Paul. *The Social Transformation of American Medicine.* Basic Books, 1982.

Stigler, James and James Heibert. "Improving Mathematics Teaching". *Educational Leadership,* (Feb. 2004).

Stipek, D. and D. Daniels. "Declining Perceptions of Competence: A Consequence of Changes in the Child or in the Educational Environment?" *Journal of Educational Psychology,* 80 (1988): 352-356.

Stone, C. L. "A Meta-Analysis of Advanced Organizer Studies." *Journal of Experimental Education* 51(7) (1983): 194-199.

Tappan, M. B. "Sociocultural Psychology and Caring Pedagogy: Exploring Vygotsky's 'Hidden Curriculum'". *Educational Psychologist,* 33(1) (1998): 23-33.

Taylor, Barbara, P., David Pearson, Kathleen F. Clark, and Sharon Walpole. "Effective Schools / Accomplished Teachers." *The Reading Teacher* 53 (Oct.1999): 156-159.

__________. "Effective Schools and Accomplished Teachers: Lessons About Primary Grade Reading Instruction in Low Income Schools." *The Elementary School Journal* 101 (2000): 121-165.

Thernstrom, Abigail, and Stephen Thernstrom. *No Excuses: Closing the Racial Gap in Learning.* New York: Simon & Schuster, 2003.

Tobin, K. and W. Capie. "Relationships Between Classroom Process Variables and Middle-School Science Achievement." *Journal of Educational Psychology* 74 (1982): 441-454.

Toole, J. C., and Karen Seashore. "The Role of Professional Learning Communities in International Education." Center for Applied Research and Educational Improvement, University of Minnesota, 2001.

Trammel, D. L., P. J. Scloss, and S. Alper. "Using Self-Recording and Graphing to Increase Completion of Homework Assignments." *Journal of Learning Disabilities* 27(2) (1994): 75-81.

Traub, James. "What No School Can Do". *The New York Times.* January 16, 2000.

Turner, J. C. "The Influence of Classroom Contexts on Young Children's Motivation for Literacy." *Reading Research Quarterly* 30 (1995): 410-441.

Tyler, Ralph. *Basic Principles of Curriculum and Instruction.* Chicago: University of Chicago Press, 1949.

U. S. Federal Government Budget 2003. www.gpoacess.gov/usbudget/fy03/pdf/bud34.pdf

VanOverwalle, F., K. Segebarth, and M. Goldschstein. "Improving Performance of Freshmen Through Attributional Testimonies from Fellow Students." *British Journal of Educational Psychology* 59 (1989): 75-85.

Walker, Hill M., Elizabeth Ramsey, and Frank M. Gresham. "Heading Off Disruptive Behavior". *American Educator,* Winter 2003/2004:6 - ?

Waxman, H. J. "Productive Teaching." In H. C. Waxman and H. J. Walberg (Eds.) *New Directions for Teaching Practice and Research,* 75-104. Berkeley: McCutchen Publishing Corporation, 1999.

Weinstein, C. and R. Mayer. "The Teaching of Learning Strategies." In M.C. Wittrock (Ed.), *Handbook of Research on Teaching* (3rd ed.). New York: Macmillan, 1986.

Welch, M. "Students' Use of Three-Dimensional Modeling While Designing and Making a Solution to a Technical Problem." Paper presented at the annual meeting of the American Educational Research Association, Chicago, April 1997.

West, Lucy, and Fritz C. Staub. *Content-Focused Coaching: Transforming Mathematics Lessons.* Pittsburgh: Heinemann, 2003.

Wiggins, G. and J. McTighe. *Understanding by Design.* Alexandria: ASCD, 1998.

Willoughby, T., S. Desmarias, E. Wood, S. Sims, and M. Kalra. "Mechanisms That Facilitate the Effectiveness of Elaboration Strategies." *Journal of Educational Psychology* 89(4) (1997): 682-685.

Wise, Arthur E. "Teaching Teams" Education Week, Vol. 24, No. 5. Sept. 29, 2004: 44.

Wise, K. C., and J. R. Okey. "A Meta-Analysis of the Effects of Various Science Teaching Strategies on Achievement." *Journal of Research in Science Teaching* 20(5) (1983): 415-425.

Zimmerman, B.J. and R. Blotner. "Effects of Model Persistence and Success on Children's Problem Solving." *Journal of Educational Psychology* 71 (1979): 508-513.

Bibliography for Professional Learning Communities

Berliner, David C. and Biddle, Bruce J., *The Manufactured Crisis.* Reading, MA: Addison-Wesley Publishing Co., 1995.

Block, N.J., and Gerald Dworkin, eds. *The IQ Controversy: Critical Readings*. New York: Pantheon, 1976.

Bryk, A. & Schneider, B. *Trust in Schools: A Core Resource for Improvement.* New York: The Russell Sage Foundation, 2002.

Chapman, P.D. *Schools As Sorters*. New York: New York University Press, 1988.

Dweck, C. S., & Leggett, E. L. "A Social-Cognitive Approach to Motivation and Personality". *Psychological Review*, 95(2), 256-273 (1988)

Gould, Steven Jay. *The Mismeasure of Man*. New York: W.W. Norton, 1981 and 1996.

Gross, S. "Final Report, Mathematics Content/Connections Elementary Science in Montgomery County (Maryland): A Comprehensive Transformation of a System-wide Science Program." July 1999 (Published by Montgomery County Public Schools).

Howard, J. & R. Hammond. "Rumors of Inferiority". *The New Republic*, 17-21 (1985).

Joyce, Bruce and Beverly Showers. *Student Achievement Through Staff Development*, second edition. White Plains, N.Y.: Longmans. 1995.

Keiffer-Barone, Susan, and Kathleen Ware. "Organize Teams of Teachers". *Journal of Staff Development* (Summer 2002).

Little, J.W. "Norms of Collegiality and Experimentation: Workplace Conditions of School Success." American Educational Research Journal, Fall 1982. EJ 275 511.

Mendro, Robert; Karen Bebry. "School Evaluation: A Change in Perspective". Paper presented at the Annual Meeting of the American Educational Research Association (New Orleans, LA, April 24-28, 2000).

Mensh, E & Mensh, H. *The IQ Mythology*. Carbondale and Edwardsville: Southern University Press: 1991.

Mortimore, P. P. Sammons, L. Stoll, D. Lewis and R. Ecob. *School Matters.* Somerset Wells: Open Books, 1988.

Muijs, R., D. Reynolds. "Effective Mathematics Teaching: Year 2 of a Research Project". Paper presented at the International Conference on School Effectiveness and School Improvement, Hong Kong August 2000.

Newmann, Fred M. and Gary G. Wehlage. *Successful School Restructuring*. Madison, Wisconsin: Center on Organization and Restructuring of Schools, 1995.

Ogbu, J. U. "Minority Education and Caste: The American System in Cross-Cultural Perspective". *The Crisis*, 86. 17-21 (1979).

Osborne, J.W. "Race and Academic Disidentification". *Journal of Educational Psychology*, 89(4), 728-735 (1997).

Perkins, David. *Outsmarting IQ: The Emerging Science of Learnable Intelligence.* New York: The Free Press, 1995.

Resnick, L. "From Aptitude to Effort: A New Foundation for Our Schools". *Daedalus* 124(4), 55-62 (Fall 1995).

Rosenholtz, S.J. *Teachers' Workplace: The Social Organization of Schools.* New York: Longmans, 1989.

Rosenholtz, S.J. "Workplace Conditions That Affect Teacher Quality and Commitment; Implications for Teacher Induction Programs," *Elementary School Journal,* 89/4, 421 – 449 (March 1989).

Sanders, W.L. and J.C. Rivers. "Cumulative and Residual Effects of Teachers on Future Student Academic Achievement." Knoxville, TN: University of Tennessee Value-Added Research and Assessment Center, 1996.

Snow, R.E., and E Yalow. "Education and Intelligence." In R.J. Sternberg (Ed.), *Handbook of Human Intelligence* (193-585). Cambridge, England: Cambridge University Press, 1982.

Steele, C.M. "Race and the Schooling of Black Americans". *The Atlantic Monthly* 68-78 (April 1992).

Toole, J. C. and Karen Seashore. "The Role of Professional Learning Communities in International Education." Center for Applied Research and Educational Improvement, U. of Minn., 2001.

Tyler, R. *Basic Principles of Curriculum and Instruction.* Chicago: University of Chicago Press, 1949.

Wright, S., P. Horn, and W.L. Sanders. "Teacher and Classroom Context Effects on Student Achievement: Implications for Teacher Evaluation". *Journal of Personnel Evaluation in Education,* 1997, 57-67.

Key Works on Professional Community - in chronological order

Rutter, Michael and others. Fifteen Thousand Hours: Secondary Schools and Their Effects on Children. Cambridge: Harvard University Press, 1979.

Little, J.W. "Norms of Collegiality and Experimentation: Workplace Conditions of School Success." *American Educational Research Journal*, Fall 1982. EJ 275 511.

Purkey, Stewart C. and Smith, S. Marshall. "Effective Schools: A Review." *The Elementary School Journal*, March 1983. EJ 281 542.

Goodlad, John. *A Place Called School: Prospects for the Future*. New York: McGraw-Hill, 1984.

Saphier, J.D. and M. King. "Good Seeds Grow in Strong Cultures." *Educational Leadership*, March 1985.

Mortimore, P., Sammons, P., Stoll, L., Lewis, D., and Ecob, R. *School Matters: The Junior Years*. London: Open Books, 1988.

Rosenholtz, Susan. *Teachers' Workplace: The Social Organization of Schools*. New York: Longman, 1989.

Little, Judith Warren. "The Persistence of Privacy: Autonomy and Initiative in Teachers Professional Relations." *Teachers College Record*, 91, 509-536, 1990.

Heifitz, R.A. and Donald L.Laurie. "The Work of Leadership." *Harvard Business Review*, Dec. 2001.

Hopkins, David. "Integrating Staff Development and School Improvement: A Study of Teacher Personality and School Climate." In Bruce Joyce Ed., *Changing School Culture Through Staff Development*. Alexandria, VA: ASCD, 1990.

Joyce, Bruce and Beverly Showers. *Student Achievement Through Staff Development*, 2nd ed. White Plains, N.Y.: Longman Publishers, 1995.

Newmann, Fred M. and Wehlage, Gary G. *Successful School Restructuring*. Madison, Wisconsin: Center on Organization and Restructuring of Schools, 1995.

Louis, Karen Seashore and Sharon D. Kruse. *Professionalism and Community*. Thousand Oaks: Corwin Press, 1995.

Resnick, Lauren. "From Aptitude to Effort: A New Foundation for Our Schools." *Daedalus*, 124(4), 1995, 55-62.

Newmann, Fred M. and Associates. *Authentic Achievement*. San Francisco: Jossey Bass, 1996.

Elmore, Richard and Deanna Burney. "Staff Development and Instructional Improvement, Community District 2, New York City." New York: National Commission on Teaching and America's Future, March 1996.

Resnick, Lauren. "Institute for Learning: Instruction and Learning Profile v2.1." University of Pittsburgh, 1997.

Putnam, Ralph T. and Hilda Borko. "Chapter 13: Teacher Learning: Implications of New Views of Cognition." B.J. Biddle et al (eds.), *International Handbook of Teachers and Teaching*. Amsterdam: Kluwer Academic Publishers, 1997. 1223-1296.

Deal, Terrence E. and Kent D. Peterson. *Shaping School Culture.* San Francisco: Jossey Bass, 1999.

Schmoker, Mike. *Results: The Key to Continuous Improvement*. Alexandria, Va.: A.S.C.D., 1999.

Elmore, Richard F. "Leadership for Large-Scale Improvement in American Education". Unpublished paper, September 1999.

Joyce, Bruce, Emily Calhoun, David Hopkins. *The New Structure of School Improvement.* Philadelphia: Open University Press. 1999.

Langer, Judith A. "Excellence in English in Middle and High School: How Teachers' Professional Lives Support Student Achievement." *American Educational Research Journal*, Vol. 37, No. 2 Summer 2000 397-439.

Toole, J. C. and Karen Seashore. "The Role of Professional Learning Communities in International Education." Center for Applied Research and Educational Improvement, U. of Minn., 2001.

ESSAY 2

The Significance of the Geographical State and the Ten Processes of Education Reform

Executive Summary: Fix the Broken Supply Chain

The central problem in American education is a personnel problem: the supply chain for the teacher and leader workforce is disregarded, disconnected and dysfunctional. Thus, we do not have enough teachers with enough teaching expertise to reach all our children or enough leaders with enough capacity to build high functioning teams. This is especially visible in schools serving children of poverty. Since teaching expertise is the *most significant variable in student achievement*, these personnel problems are a cap to all other improvement efforts.

You can't fix a problem if you don't define it properly. The problems in our schools cannot be fixed by working on school structure, on school governance, on school accountability, on school privatization, or on school size. It is not even primarily a matter of school funding.

The central issue is this: there is a common core of knowledge about teaching and learning for good professional practice that gets results for students. Large segments of it are missing in action from each of the ten subsystems that form the supply chain for our teacher workforce. No one is accountable for seeing it even shows up in these sub-systems, much less in an integrated way. This is eminently fixable; but only if we redefine the problem and radically refocus our resources. (The same can be said for the knowledge and skills of school leadership.)

The ten sub-systems of the educator workforce supply chain are:

1. University preparation programs
2. State licensing requirements
3. School district hiring processes
4. School district induction programs
5. School district supervision and evaluation systems
6. School district professional development systems
7. State recertification requirements
8. School district salary, promotion and advancement policies
9. Individual school working conditions and structure
10. Individual school organizational culture

These ten operate collectively as a SYSTEM that produces the teacher and leader workforce we have today. They need to be yoked together and integrated with one another. Since they aren't, the work force we have today is exactly what the system is designed to produce—random pockets of high quality and large numbers of under-prepared and under-skilled teachers. There's nothing wrong with most of the *people* we have. And legions of our 3 million educators manage to function personally at a high professional level anyway. But there are also legions who don't, and it's not their fault. They work in a broken system. Fix the system. State law, state policy, and local commitments of school boards have a significant influence on all ten of these subsystems. Seven of them can be reshaped at the district level alone with insight, ability and will. Good legislation and state policy could kick-start all ten.

••••••••••••••••••••••••••••••••••••

The Ten Processes of the Personnel System

In *Reengineering the Corporation* (1993), Hammer and Champy make the point that efforts for improvement classically focus on tasks, jobs, people, and structures, but not on processes, and that as a result reform programs often fail or matter little. This has been true in 20th Century Educational Reform efforts as well.

The previous essay made the point that teaching expertise is the highest leverage and the missing focus of educational reform. There are ten processes, ten levers if you will, to push if we are to systematically improve teaching expertise:

1. Process for Teacher Education
2. Process for Teacher Licensing and Certification in Each State
3. Process for Recruitment and Hiring
4. Process for Teacher Induction in a Teacher's First District
5. Process for Teacher Continuing Education and Professional Development
6. Process for Determining and Meeting Standards of Teacher Performance (Teacher Evaluation Systems)
7. Process for Recertification
8. Process for Teacher Advancement
9. Process of Structuring the Workplace for Professional Working Conditions
10. Process of Building a Growth Oriented Culture in the Workplace for Adults

The ten processes above have great influence over teacher learning, teacher capacity, and teacher efficacy. What we need to do is *tie these ten processes together, align them with one another* if we wish to wind up with high capacity teachers for all our nation's children. This is to say that the formula for success in improving schools is to approach all ten processes for increasing teacher capacity *together and simultaneously* with an integrated cohesive plan so that each system or process reinforces the effectiveness of the others.

Ten Processes That Influence Teaching Expertise

(What Ties Them Together is the Map of Pedagogical Knowledge)

1. **Teacher Education (Graduate and Undergraduate)**
2. **Licensing and Certification**
3. **Recruiting and Hiring**
4. **Induction**
5. **Continuing Education and Professional Development**
6. **Teacher Evaluation**
7. **Recertification**
8. **Teacher Advancement**
9. **Structure of the Workplace**
10. **Culture of the School and Professional Community**

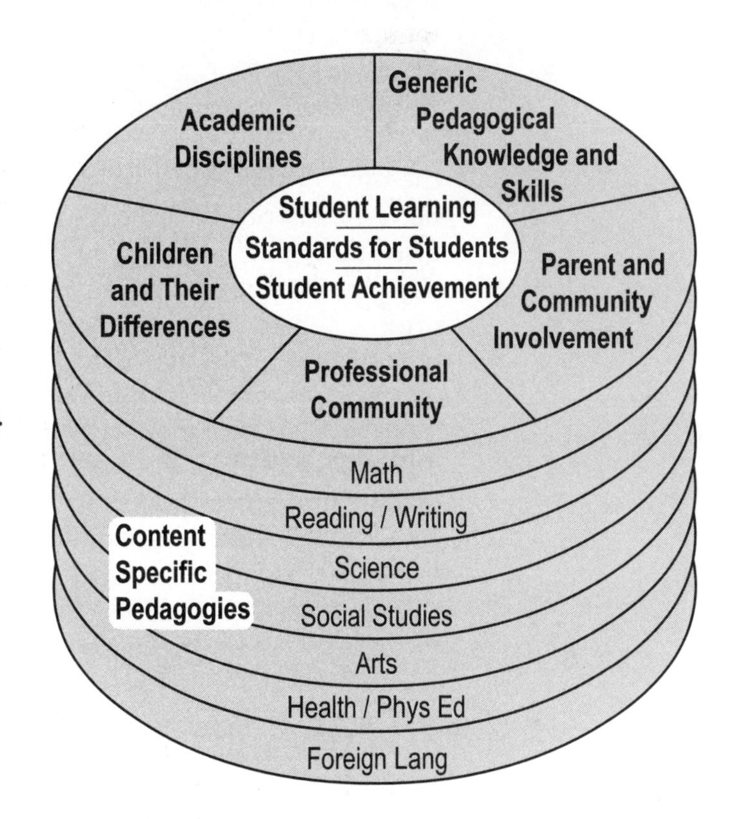

Research for Better Teaching and ***TEACHERS*[21]**

The smallest unit in which this kind of integrated change effort can take place is the state. The geographical state, not the individual school and not the district will be the operational unit of enduring change—emphasize *enduring*—in American education. I am not talking narrowly about the State Department of Education here, but the state as a *geographical unit and a system of districts operating* within certain structures, a few of which are, indeed, primarily influenced and controlled by the State Department of Education.

It is, of course, true that the school and the district is where the action takes place. That is where improvement is visible and only there do we see effects on children. The argument of this essay is that school and district change does not *endure* unless it is supported by elements in the larger system that surround it; and the smallest viable unit size in which to build the supports for enduring change is the governmental unit we call a state.

I will argue that the proposition above is true because the changes that affect teacher learning and knowledge in an enduring way are rooted in statewide practices and systems and also in State law and regulations. They *could* also be rooted in statewide collaboratives with strong ties and commitments between districts—somewhat antithetical to the individualistic ways American school districts participate in collaboratives now. Instead of interacting like trading partners at the rural outpost, an ethos I would propose guides the relationships between districts in today's collaboratives (and between districts and universities, too), districts need to be more strongly interdependent... actually dependent on one another. They need to operate from the understanding that they are part of a larger "system" that influences what teachers know, believe, and can do through the ten processes.[17]

Successful changes are, indeed, actualized through districts and schools. They often originate there, but history has shown that they rarely can be preserved there. The rotation of school boards and the career moves of key leaders in the ranks of teachers and administrators make restructuring and improvement efforts at the school and district level vulnerable to the gigantic back pressure that the "ten processes" currently exert *against* reform, not in behalf of it. The way we have been going about educational reform in this century is tantamount to trying to grow lilies in the desert: the ecosystem doesn't support the garden, even if we get a few plants to live for a while with intensive tending.

Because we have failed to see the significance of the state as a system that includes districts, universities, and collaboratives as well as the regulatory Department of Education, we have doomed wonderful school and district improvement programs to short lives. It is time to "reengineer" our concept of reform and focus on the state as the unit of change and the ten processes as the instrumentalities of enduring reform.

In the previous essay, I made the case that we have a huge professional knowledge base on which to base successful practice; we have, however, failed to acknowledge it and failed to build it into rigorous performance assessments for licensure, certification and recertification. The purpose of that essay was to profile the knowledge base and argue that the most significant (and most neglected) lever on school improvement is to make teaching a true and rigorous profes-

[17] This might be accomplished through State sponsored collaboratives such as the B.O.C.E.S. structure in New York State.

sion based on knowledge and skill. In this essay, we are playing that recommendation out.

Base each of the ten processes that affect teacher quality in the knowledge and skill of the profession, and then align them with one another across a state. This means aligning legislation, state policy, university education, and district practice with a knowledge-based view of proficient teaching. And it means doing so planfully for each of the following processes.

1. Teacher Education

Given the complexity of the knowledge and skill required for successful teaching, it would be as unrealistic to expect university graduates to be prepared to teach as it would to expect medical school graduates to commence independent practice of medicine. They simply don't know enough. In education it is even worse, because we expect candidates to be acquiring the rudiments of a liberal education at the same time as preparing for professional practice. Candidates for teaching need a minimum of a fifth year with intensive focus on planning and curriculum skills and a specialization in teaching their academic area. For example, the technology of teaching primary grade literacy is very sophisticated. And children in disadvantaged communities need beginning teachers who can land in the classroom running with these teaching skills. A liberal arts college education followed by an intensive year of preparation in content-specific pedagogy is a bare minimum of preparation. Missing is the essential foundation of classroom management, which cannot be learned in the university classroom. One's first year of teaching should be an internship year in which one is placed with a team of teachers and paced through the formal steps of creating classroom climate, setting limits, learning the body language of meaning business (Jones 2000), and creating meaningful school-home communication. Most important of all, graduation from such programs must be marked by successful passage through performance-based assessments where the candidates have to show, by actual performance, that they have competence at the relevant teaching skills.

The curriculum and assessments within teacher education institutions need to be congruent with the standards for knowledge-based practiced referenced above. Currently they are not. There is no agreement across teacher education institutions about what graduates should know or be able to do to enter classrooms as competent novices. Hence, there is no consistency across teacher education institutions about the experience candidates have. Upgraded certification for teacher training institutions (National Council for Accreditation for Teacher Education—NCATE) is a force in this direction, but is meeting strong opposition from many institutions that wrongly see the teacher standards movement as a threat to their autonomy. The time has come for this to end. The voice of the state legislature can be brought to bear through the higher education approval process by which each teacher training institutions' charters are renewed. *Teacher training institutions can be required to make their programs reflect the common knowledge base and be performance-based.*

2. Teacher Licensing and Certification

The process of teacher licensing and certification has begun to change in the U.S. — and it is about time. The licensing process for any profession establishes standards for knowledge-based practice upon which public trust is ultimately based. Doctors must be board certified; lawyers must pass the bar; but teachers don't need to demonstrate specific knowledge or skills to practice. Teacher licensing and certification in the U.S. has been based on passive criteria throughout this century — meaning one doesn't have to prove one can do *anything* at the performance level to get a license. One has only to passively survive seat time and finish courses. The national movement for professionalization is seeing the creation of independent state licensing boards[18], national standards for beginning teachers (Interstate New Teacher Assessment and Support Consortium—INTASC) and accomplished teachers (National Board of Professional Teaching Standards—NBPTS). We are also seeing legislated state performance standards that all districts must apply in their teacher evaluation systems (Massachusetts). Of the ten processes described in this essay, this one is receiving the most attention and making slow but steady progress.

But we are still far from a standard that calls for performance-based assessment to get a license to teach. Connecticut had the most developed program in the 1990s where external assessors, operating with state funding, visited the classes of beginning teachers and assessed their proficiency by actual observation of performance. The assessors were well trained and the assessment instrument was knowledge-based and well structured to collect data on teacher decision making

[18] 11 states now have independent licensing boards: California, Oregon, Minnesota, Nevada, Iowa, Kentucky, Georgia, Indiana, Wyoming, N. Dakota, W. Virginia. Source: National Council for Accreditation of Teacher Education, Washington, D.C.

from repertoires of skills rather than implementation of "effective" behaviors. Observation by state assessors using the Connecticut model is not the only way, but it is certainly a rigorous way to structure licensure. And it is part of a 15-year commitment that the state has made to developing workforce excellence. The payoff, incidentally, has been among the best test score gains in the nation despite increase in number of children living in poverty and number of children from diverse language backgrounds.

3. Recruitment and Hiring

False starts abound for making the recruitment and hiring process more effective at attracting and retaining high quality teachers. Signing bonuses; TV ads that highlight the inspirational effects of good teachers; alternative (easier) certification programs that bring career changers into the classroom with minimum requirements (and minimum teaching skills). These approaches fail because they do not address the two key issues: working conditions and support for developing expertise.

Support

Beginners flock to districts that can offer comprehensive induction programs, districts that showed an aspiring teacher that they will not be overloaded with a stripped room, too many preps, and the most problem laden students (a common experience); districts that can show they will provide on-going seminars, coaching, and problem solving help for novices; districts that can show they value mentoring by making the criteria selective and the training rigorous (Saphier, Aschheim, and Freedman 2001).

Better salaries are not irrelevant to this picture, as Dallas and New York both found when they eliminated their teacher shortages in a stroke with pay hikes (2002). But as personnel directors are discovering, applicants are shopping for districts that will support them, and they know what to ask for.

Working Conditions

The working conditions that attract quality candidates are working conditions that have true professional characteristics that are described in other parts of this essay: joint work, shared responsibility, high opportunity for professional learning, and differentiated career options.

When we are attracting more qualified people to apply for teaching positions, then the hiring process can use technologies such as Haberman's (1995) for identifying beginners who are willing to persevere and believe in the capacity of all their children to learn despite disadvantages. This and other key beliefs can become part of hiring processes that are much more knowledge-based and tied to demonstration of performance.

4. Teacher Induction

Quality induction programs for new teachers are rare in the United States. We still plunge novice teachers into the water without adequate preparation or adequate support. Thus we lose 50% to 60% of new people within five years (Grissmer and Kirby 1987, 93, 94) and an even high percentage of entering teachers under the age of 24. Results from the California Beginning Teacher Program show that retention can go above 90% and student learning is positively impacted immediately when induction programs are thoughtful and long term (Garmston and Gless 1993). Elements to address in a complete teacher induction program would include screening and hiring procedures (Haberman 1995), rigorous mentor training, and placement of newly hired teachers in high functioning teams where the newcomers become enculturated to professional norms of collegiality, collaboration, accountability, and constant learning (Saphier 1994.) Comprehensive induction programs would include more than mentoring and enlist the whole faculty in having a stake in the beginning teacher's success, along with a belief that they all had something to offer (Saphier et al. 2001). State law would require comprehensive induction programs be developed by each district and state Department of Education would provide technical assistance on how to design and staff such programs. State legislatures would make it a priority to provide supplementary funding to districts to support these programs. Since there are few investments with more leverage to secure and retain quality teachers than good induction programs, these funding packages would remain intact even in hard budget times when other cuts had to be made.

5. Teacher Development

Teacher development is random, individualistic, and sadly inequitable across the country. Adequate and equitable teacher development would be based in part on a common map of professional knowledge (see Essay 1) held in common by licensing boards, institutions of higher learning, and school districts. Using this map as an organizer, Regional Collaboratives or Centers would make available to teachers and administrators the resources for professional study and individual skill development that individual districts, especially small and poor districts, cannot and do not offer today. They would offer inviting centers for teachers to share their Personal Practical Knowledge (see section 8 on Culture of the Workplace.)

Creating regional networks or accessible resources — ideas, things, and people — is absolutely essential and sadly missing. With some notable local exceptions most areas of the country are barren of coordinated and networked resources for teacher learning that approach equity. This is an area where federal funding could play a very constructive role.

6. Standards for Teacher and Administrator Performance

The development of standards is well underway and has been profiled under the "Teacher Certification" section above. The process I want to consider here is teacher and administrator evaluation as performed in school districts. These processes can be designed to either foster or impede learning and capacity-building for professional educators. In many districts they are, at best, neutral; that is, they have no great effect either positive or negative on teacher and administrator learning: they are pro forma processes that absorb time and consume forest products. In some districts, teacher evaluation systems clearly obstruct teacher learning by (1) devaluing teaching by paying scant attention to evaluation; (2) attempting to quantify teaching with checklists and scores; (3) putting teachers in competition with one another through merit pay schemes; and (4) creating a culture of inspection and mistrust by poorly designed evaluation systems.

But evaluation systems can be constructed to actively sponsor teacher (and administrator) learning; and they can do so in a way that does not dodge the need for organizations to be able to identify and respond decisively to unsatisfactory performance. Such processes emphasize multiple year Professional Growth Cycles (Saphier 1993) where traditional "evaluation" is done only once every three of four years (see Essay 3) though an administrator can put a particular teacher into the evaluation year at any time if there are concerns. In such an evaluation system there are no "years off". In years when formal evaluation by administrators is not done, teachers are required to choose from a menu of rigorous options for professional growth, do goal setting, plan projects, and report on their learning progress at the end of the year. In some districts these reports go to panels of peers, not to administrators. In other districts frequent peer observation is required in one of years between evaluations.

During the evaluation year itself, a growth-oriented process produces detailed data-oriented observation notes and narrative write-ups, no ratings, rankings, or points that add up to a teacher "grade". And administrators, who have far fewer teachers to evaluate in a given year, can observe more frequently and use good coaching skills where appropriate—which is most of the time—to assist teachers in analyzing their lessons and making plans based on data about how the lessons went (Costa and Garmston 1994). All the same principles should be applied to processes for evaluation of administrators. To be certified as an administrator, an individual should have to show by performance that they have proficiency at the skills above. This is, once again, a key lever of the state on influencing teacher quality. Finally, student results should be included in a responsible way in teacher evaluation systems (see Essay 3).

7. Recertification

We have already made the case for performance-based certification tied to the main categories of the knowledge base. Recertification is a process maintained by true professions in which members must show they have maintained their skills (airline pilots) or have updated and expanded their knowledge and skill (medical doctors). Either approach would be appropriate for teachers. We recommend the latter through the satisfaction of a distribution requirement every 5 years. To be recertified, teachers would have to show they had added an increment of knowledge or skill to their repertoires in each of the six areas of professional knowledge profiled in essay one. State PDP or course credit systems tied to performance assessment in the courses could be adapted to meet these requirements.

8. Teacher Advancement

In a fully aligned system, the process for moving up the ladder in teaching would give incentive for educators to learn new skills. We are some distance from being able to set this redesigned process in motion. The first part of the process, the development of performance assessments for teachers and administrators, is on the action agenda in many states at the current time. And precedents exist already for such assessments as the Connecticut Competency Instrument (CCI) and the National Principals' Assessment Centers (Hersey 1986).

"Skill-based pay" is already an operating process in certain industries (Firestone 1994) and is being piloted in a few school districts ("Excellent Teachers Rewarded" 1995). In skill-based pay, people get raises when they show evidence they have acquired new skills or capacities. As opposed to evaluation-based merit pay, which pits educators against each other to beat out their peers in competition for a limited pot of "merit" money, skill-based pay is tied to authentic performance assessments and gives teachers incentives for increasing their capacity; and it does so from a level playing field where all have equal opportunity to be rewarded for investing in their own efficacy. Skill-based pay is not a zero sum game where only a few can win at the expense of others.

But "advancement" should mean more than pay raises. The absence of positions to aspire toward in teaching (i.e., positions of increased responsibility requiring experience, judgment and high levels of specialized skills) saps the initiative of many senior people in education and causes others to leave. This is the place to bring back creative proposals of the 80s (Devaney 1987) for positions such as Lead Teacher and to add others: for example, Mentors with high levels of training and significant responsibility in new teacher induction programs; or Team Leaders who have superior skills in curriculum design and development. In this role, individuals would be responsible for curriculum integration efforts across grade level teams, within middle school teams, and for high school teachers who share common courses. With the great wave of new teachers coming into the business over the next decade and the attendant cost savings as 2/3 of our high salary teachers retire, *the money is already in school district budgets to create these positions.*

9. Workplace Structure – particularly schedules and groupings of teachers and students

Teachers' opportunity for learning is significantly influenced by working closely and collaboratively with colleagues to deliver daily instruction. Physical proximity does not do it; doing joint work with colleagues does (Little 1988). This joint work can take the form of side by side team teaching (the best form of teaming in my opinion) It can take the form of co-development of assessment tasks and rubrics to use in common with students. It can take the form of designing and implementing integrated curriculum for a joint group of students. But for any of this to happen, the organization of time (long blocks in high schools) and the grouping of students and teachers into teams jointly responsible for the progress of the youngsters is essential.

10. Culture of the Workplace

> "Overall, if we compared two average students, one in a school with low professional community, and the other in a school with high professional community, the students in the high community would score about 27% higher on the SRS measure. The difference would represent a gain of 31 percentile points."
>
> – Newmann and Wehlage

In the 1990s, powerful research showed beyond question that schools that succeeded for children, especially poor urban children, had strong organizational cultures (see bibliography). As more and more work was done to understand these cultures, they came to be called Professional Learning Communities. The reason Professional Learning Communities (PLC) increase student learning is that they produce more good teaching by more teachers more of the time. Put simply, PLC improves teaching, which improves student results, especially for the least advantaged students.

It is, therefore, particularly important to understand what these cultures are like and how they are created. This was the focus of Big Rock #2 in the previous essay.

We have already made the case that the prime characteristic of powerful relationships is honest, open communication where conflict can happen in healthy ways, out in the open, and where the undiscussable can be made discussable. This position in the literature is well represented by such authors as Michael Fullan and others who write about the importance of collaboration.

The type of collaboration found in strong professional communities means a lot more than working cooperatively with others on committees or at meetings. It means five specific observable norms among staff members:

- High frequency of teacher talk about teaching in increasingly concrete and precise language
- High frequency of teachers observing one another
- High frequency of teachers making materials and planning lessons together
- Teachers teaching each other about the practice of teaching (Little 1982)
- Teachers willing to ask for and provide one another with assistance (Rosenholtz 1989)

Together, these five observable patterns define "Collegiality," now a word in our professional vocabulary with precise meaning.

Professional isolation carries profound consequences for teachers' opportunities to learn and solve classroom problems. "However, to the extent that teachers believe that anyone, even the most capable colleague, might need help in a similar situation, it becomes unnecessary for them to draw causal inferences about their own teaching inadequacy. That is, if teaching is collectively viewed as an inherently difficult undertaking, it is both necessary and legitimate to seek and to offer professional assistance. This is exactly what occurs in instructionally successful schools, where, because of strong administrative or faculty leadership, *teaching is considered a collective rather than an individual enterprise* (italics not in original); requests and offers of assistance among colleagues are frequent, and reasoned intentions, informed choices, and collective actions set the conditions under which teachers improve instructionally." (op.cit.)

High stakes tests have invited, if not forced, another behavior into the domain of collaborative work: systematic examination of data about student performance, and further, systematic examination of student work itself. This joint practice is so important we have included it as a separate norm in our map of professional community (Essay 1, p. 32). The analysis is done together by teachers of common academic content. It should become the starting point for the concrete talk about teaching, the planning and making of materials together, and the peer observation that comprise Little's definition of "collegiality".

Rosenholtz's findings challenge us to invent structures, reserve time on agendas of existing structures, and build a behavioral norm of asking for help and of taking the risk of giving it too. Contemplating what such a norm would be like brings us to the final point about PLC: how comfortable do we feel being honest with one another about our feelings, about our doubts, and about our disagreements? Do our relationships allow us to make the undiscussable discussable? Now we are beyond the structures and the protocols for teacher talk. We are into the D.N.A. of powerful professional learning communities and the quality of conversations between staff members. Are they courageous?

If this is the right cast for what school culture is, (or its 21st century update, Professional Learning Community) then we need to act on it. We already know that schools with strong Professional Learning Communities improve instruction rapidly and thus, get better student results. Building and strengthening these features of the school organization and its human environment constitutes the main job of leadership. Therefore, the education, certification, and evaluation of leaders must de designed around how to lead in this way — the knowledge and skills of cultural leadership. And that has been the point of this section.

Alignment at the State Level

It is easy to conjure a vision of these ten systems operating in alignment with one another. It is yet another thing to design a change process to *get* them in alignment. Let's look at the vision first. The vision:

Teacher Certification and Teacher Education

State teacher certification requirements, administered through the Department of Education, are knowledge-based and granted through performance assessment keyed to the INTASC standards. The performance assessments are complex, multifaceted, and demanding. Teacher education programs have aligned themselves with the requirements so their graduates are prepared for meeting entry level standards. Part of teachers' assessed knowledge includes how to act as a positive force for school culture building.

The scenario above contains three aligned processes: Certification; University education; Culture of the workplace.

Teacher Induction

High quality three year induction programs are available for new teachers in all districts. Large districts train their own mentors. Small districts have equally well trained mentors who are educated and supported through regional collaboratives, perhaps subsidized by the state (and in a future life, by the federal government.) New teachers are placed for one to three years in special induction schools. These induction schools are organized with the attributes described below under "Workplace Structure." Continuous learning experiences are provided to new teachers formally and informally through district resources and the Regional Center for Professional Teaching Knowledge.

The scenario above contains four aligned processes: Induction; Culture of the Workplace; Teacher and Administrator Development; Workplace Structures

Teacher and Administrator Development

The state Department of Education has provided startup funding and organizational resources for Regional Centers for Professional Teaching Knowledge. These electronically networked Regional Centers for Professional Teaching Knowledge make available on-line to every teacher (and administrator) in the region two kinds of downloadable resources: (1) lessons, materials, analogies, tasks, rubrics, samples of student work for teaching specific concepts or areas of content; (2) digitized video segments illustrating the items in (1) as well as illustrating trans-disciplinary teaching techniques (e.g., classroom management moves; instructional strategies like how to do "reciprocal teaching," etc...) (3) an index of human resources within the region ... i.e., names of people with times and places where workshops, study groups, or seminars are being offered; names of people who are willing to offer other kinds of learning experiences (e.g., teaching a demonstration lesson in your class or having you visit to witness a demo lesson in their class).

The map of professional knowledge from which the "Center" operates is congruent with the framework of the National Board of Professional Teaching Standards and actively represents a view of professional knowledge as "repertoire" and "matching," not "effective behaviors" (Saphier, 1994). This more professional view of teaching knowledge acts to support the culture of collegiality, collaboration, and constant learning that ground the healthy workplace culture described below.

The scenario above contains two aligned processes: Teacher and Administrator Development and Culture of the Workplace.

Teacher Advancement

Salary raises are tied to two processes: (1) demonstrated mastery through performance assessment of new knowledge-based teaching skills, and (2) extra pay for extra responsibility in a differentiated position such as Mentor Teacher, Team Leader, Curriculum Leader...

The scenario above contains four aligned processes: Teacher and Administrator Development; Teacher Standards; Teacher Advancement; Workplace Structure.

Teacher and Administrator Standards

Individual district teacher evaluation systems are nested in a Professional Growth Cycle where the emphasis is on professional growth; yet a clear, decisive, fair performance-based accountability system exists for identifying and dealing with sub-standard teaching. Administrators are trained through the state Leadership Academy, and accountable in their districts for implementing this evaluation system. Teachers are responsible for implementing the professional growth cycle. The state standards for administrators support these practices and the state Leadership Academy offers annual training in supervision and evaluation keyed to the state standards for teacher performance.

The scenario above contains two aligned processes: Teacher Development and Teacher Standards.

Workplace Structure

Schools are small enough for personal caring and knowledge of students. Teachers are organized into teams that consider themselves jointly accountable for student results. Differentiated staffing gives senior, qualified teachers curriculum leadership and mentor responsibilities. Block scheduling and longer more flexible school days and years make possible more motivating integrated curriculum, student apprenticeships, and "reteaching loops" for students who need extra time to master rigorous material at high standards. These changes are supported by recommendations recently made by the Massachusetts State Commission on Time and Learning (1995) and the Federal Report "Prisoners of Time" (Kane 1994).

The scenario above contains three aligned processes: Induction; Teacher Advancement; Workplace Structure.

Workplace Culture/Professional Learning Community

School leaders are trained and evaluated on their ability to nurture conditions of collegiality, experimentation, and reaching out to the knowledge base by faculty. Administrators are also evaluated on their ability to support teachers taking initiative to do things for the good of the school. "Culture building" is in the state standards for administrators, built into the training delivered by the state Leadership Academy and into Degree Programs in Educational Leadership offered by universities.

The scenario above contains four aligned systems: Teacher and Administrator Standards; Workplace Culture; University Programs; Teacher and Administrator Development.

With the ten processes above aligned as described, enduring and increasing teacher capacity would impact the achievement of all learners. How do we get these ten processes aligned in congruence with the vision above? Clearly no single agency has the clout to accomplish this kind of integrated change by itself.

The vision above can only be accomplished with coordinated movement across a common front by such players as a State Licensing Board, University degree programs, regional collaboratives, the state legislature, local school boards, and decision makers in individual districts. Forging such an alliance is a political task-based on constant discussion, networking, and bringing people together from these different constituencies. Each of the ten processes has primary players and physical sites. These players need to see that their cause is common and their relationship needs to be one of interdependence and reinforcement in the way they operate.

Alignment at the District Level

A common view of the knowledge base on teaching is shared between the teacher evaluation system and the Department of Staff Development of the district. In fact, staff development is recast as career development, with a menu of offerings across the knowledge base always available either through the districts own trainers or through partnerships with regions colleges and other school districts. The induction program has been built around the components of professional knowledge most needed by beginning teachers, especially those related to classroom management, planning skills, and content focused pedagogy in literacy (literacy across the curriculum for secondary teachers in the disciplines) and math. So the map of professional knowledge serves as an anchor and developmental menu for staff development planning for all district staff members.

When hiring teachers, the Human Resources (HR) Office is tuned into knowledge-based aspects of teaching that are particularly important. For example, interviews probe a candidate's belief about innate ability vs. effort-based achievement and ask "what if" questions that assess a candidates willingness to persevere. HR is looking for people who believe in collaboration and are willing to have their teaching viewed by colleagues (Professional Community).

Because of the district's belief in the complexity and importance of teacher capacity to student achievement, it has developed and the school board funds a wide array of structures to support teacher learning including lesson study groups, intervisitation projects and professional development schools. Schools are structured and schedules are planned so these activities are possible, as well as common planning times for groups of teachers who share a grade or a subject. District policy continually focuses leaders on these priorities, as does the evaluation system for principals and department chairs.

The knowledge-based view of successful teaching has led to differentiated staffing and multiple points of entry into direct work with children, including models that resemble the Milken Family Foundation's design (1999). Teachers advance by demonstrated competence into leadership positions for supervision of grade level teachers and aides.

The in-house Leadership Academy brings many into the role of principal and assistant principal with a strong knowledge of how to build Professional Community. No one, in fact, from inside or outside the system can get a building leadership position without showing commitment and competence as a culture builder. Small districts have collaboratives to provide the services that larger districts provide through in-house academies.

The Future

While individual schools and districts can influence the seven processes that are district-based, we need a broader-based conversation among policy makers and opinion leaders through any and all forums available to us as educators. We need to talk explicitly about the interdependence and need for integration of these ten processes. Avenues include local school board information sessions; state school board meetings; state conventions of discipline-based associations; state conventions of leadership and teacher associations; university colloquia; radio talk shows; Chambers of Commerce; Rotary and other business clubs; church groups; legislative lobbying groups. Ultimately, the power of state law and the authority of state licensing boards must be in alignment with the standards for teacher and administrator performance. What we have to do is get the actors in each of the ten systems to be aware of the other systems in which they don't directly participate and cause them to see themselves as interdependent with those other systems.

School improvement is a combination of resources, insight, strategy and will. We have arguably been weak on all four.

Resources

The first premise of this essay has been that we have been dividing, even scattering, our resources for educational improvement instead of focusing on the most important lever for change — people, and increasing their capacity through knowledge. Let's focus our resources on our people, our professional educators.

Insight

Second, let us use the insight that the geographical state will be the enduring unit of change; and the state is a system of players and agencies whose efforts need to be aligned in purpose and coordinated in design to influence teacher learning.

Strategy

Third, let us use the strategy of networking and persuasive argumentation to have key players and agencies come to first understand and then contribute to and *own* a new vision of educational improvement through the ten processes.

And that leaves "will."

Do we have the will as a state (as a nation) to commit the time, energy, and resources it takes to reengineer the ten processes?

Will

There is significant evidence that the American public believes: (1) our educational system is in poor shape, (2) getting worse, and (3) that no efforts at reform are really making much difference.

Our public ignores demographic shifts, increased enrollment and graduation rates, and actual standardized test scores that counter the conventional wisdom of school decline (Koretz 1986, 92; Linn and Dunbar 1990; Bracey 1994). They lump the problems of schools with the problems of society, and become accusatory and non-supportive.

They think the productivity problems of schools are due to a combination of incompetence and mediocrity that is remediable through merit pay, competition between schools (schools of choice) and better management. "Just get some good people in there, for God sake, and put some capitalistic competition in the education market and good schools will start to emerge," goes the thinking. They believe at bottom that teaching is easy work that any literate and reasonably decent person can do well.

If we do not change this image of teaching as easy work, we will have a hard time mobilizing the public will and public commitment we need as pressure to change the ten systems. Elsewhere (Saphier 1994) I have made the case that many of us educators need to seek out skilled media partners and educate the public about the complexities of good professional teaching. We need, furthermore, to show convincingly the concrete difference it makes in people's daily lives — including senior citizens and people with no children in school[19] — if today's youngsters are working with high capacity teachers on a daily basis.

The gist of this essay is to suggest a role shift for educators who up until now have been devoting their careers to learning how to teach and administer better, and then trying to apply their new learnings with students in their own schools and districts. I, myself, have been such a person until now.

I first wrote this essay in 1993. It fell on deaf ears. What has changed since then, however, is the implementation of the standards movement, the passage of the federal law "No Child Left Behind," the demographic change to a near-majority non-white student population, and an on-rushing global economy that is leaving the United States

[19] In 1970 there were 4 million more children than adults in this country. In 1995 there were 33 million more adults than children. Source: James Pusely, Virginia Beach Public Schools.

at a competitive disadvantage for skilled workers. High stakes test and accountability have not given us the schools we want and need. Frustrated voters have increased their support of charter schools, which have not performed any better than public schools. "Programs" that seek superior approaches to instruction through teacher-proof curriculum have continued to yield null results. Now, finally, there is beginning acceptance in the conventional wisdom of the significance of good teaching and that support for good teaching is what we've left out of the picture. But who can explain what good teaching is but educators themselves who turn their attention to educating our public?

We can't stop working with children or cease working to improve our own institutions. But a great many of us need immediately to begin looking for forums to address our communities, our public, and our legislators to reeducate them about the importance and complexity of good teaching. Otherwise, even the most successful of us will each end our careers with individual accomplishments that do not impact the systems in which we worked — individual trophies, as it were, for teams that have ceased to exist or be cared about. We could do better. Instead, we could have our names on plaques commemorating the creation of new integrated processes for teacher learning that endured many generations and ultimately moved an entire country.

••••••••••••••••••••••••••••••••••••

The next essay is a case study of the implementation of many of the ideas presented so far in this monograph. It is a study of a large district with a significant urban and multi-ethnic population, Montgomery County, MD. It is, of course, an unfinished story, but it is also seven years of continuous and successful work to recognize the significance of teaching expertise and build that recognition into the operating processes of the district. The case study highlights the processes of teacher evaluation, professional development, administrator development and principal evaluation.

What will be particularly interesting to school practitioners is the enduring partnership that has been forged between the teachers' union and the school administration, and now replicated between the principals' union and the school administration, to take joint responsibility for student learning. It has been indispensable to the outstanding results this district of 192 schools is achieving and is a focus of the case study.

Bibliography

Barth, Roland. "The Principal and the Profession of Teaching." California Commission on the Teaching Profession. April 1985.

Bracey, Gerard W. "The Fourth Bracey Report on the Condition of Public Education." *Phi Delta Kappan.* vol. 76, no. 2, Oct. 1994.

Costa, Arthur and Garmston, Robert. *Cognitive Coaching: A Foundation for Renaissance Schools.* Christopher-Gordon Publishers, Norwood, MA. 1994.

Devaney, Kathleen. "The Lead Teacher: Ways to Begin." Task Force on Teaching as a Profession. Carnegie Forum on Education and th Economy. March 1987.

"Excellent Teacher Rewarded." *WCER Highlights.* Wisconsin Center for Education Research. University of Wisconsin - Madison, School of Education. vol. 7, no. 1, Spring 1995.

Firestone, William A. "Redesigning Teacher Salary Systems for Educational Reform." *American Educational Research Journal.* vol. 31, no. 3, 1994.

Fullan, Michael with Suzanne Stiegelbauer. *The New Meaning of Educational Change.* 2nd ed. New York: Teachers College Press. 1991.

Garmston, Sue and Janet Gless. "Mentoring Strategies to Empower Beginning Teachers." Presentation at ASCD Annual Conference, Washington, D.C., March 27, 1993.

Grissmer, David W. and Sheila Nataraj Kirby. *Teacher Attrition: The Uphill Climb To Staff the Nation's Schools.* Center for the Study of the Teaching Profession, RAND. Washington, D.C. August, 1987.

________. "Teacher Attrition: Theory, Evidence, and Suggested Policy Options." Paper presented at the World Bank/Harvard Institute for International Develoment Seminar on "Policies Affecting Learning Outcomes Through Impacts on Teachers." Cambridge, Mass. June 28-July 2, 1993. RAND. Santa Monica, Cal. June 1993.

Haberman, Martin. "Selecting 'Star' Teachers for Children and Youth in Urban Poverty." *Phi Delta Kappan.* vol. 76, no. 10, June 1995.

Hammer, Michael and James Champy. *Reengineering the Corporation: A Manifesto for Business Revolution.* Harper Business, New York. 1993.

Hersey, Paul. "Selecting and Developing Educational Leaders: A Search for Excellence." *NASSP Bulletin.* vol. 70, no. 486, January 1986.

Jones, Fred. *Tools for Teaching: Discipline, Instruction, Motivation.* Santa Cruz: Frederic Jones & Associates, 2000.

Kane, Cheryl. *Prisoners of Time: Research.* National Education Commission on Time and Learning. Washington, D.C., Sept. 1994.

Koretz, Daniel. "Trends in Educational Achievement." Congressional Budget Office, Washington, D.C. 1986.

Koretz, Daniel. "What Happened to Test Scores and Why?" *Educational Measurement: Issues and Practice,* 7-11. 1992.

Linn, Robert L. and Stephen B. Dunbar. "The Nation's Report Card Goes Home: Good News and Bad About Trends in Achievement." *Phi Delta Kappan,* October, 1990.

Little, Judith Warren. "Norms of Collegiality and Experimentation: Workplace Conditions of School Success." *American Educational Research Journal.* (Fall 1982).

Little, Judith Warren. *Teachers as Colleagues.* Far West Laboratory for Educational Research and Development, San Francisco, CA:1988.

Massachusetts Commission on Time and Learning. "Unlocking the Power of Time". Malden, Nov. 1995.

Mendro, Robert; Karen Bebry. "School Evaluation: A Change in Perspective". Paper presented at the Annual Meeting of the American Educational Research Association (New Orleans, LA, April 24-28, 2000).

Milken, Lowell. *A Matter of Quality: A Strategy for Assuring the High Caliber of America's Teachers.* Santa Monica: Milken Family Foundation, 1999.

Muijs, R., D. Reynolds. "Effective Mathematics Teaching: Year 2 of a Research Project". Paper presented at the International Conference on School Effectiveness and School Improvement, Hong Kong, August 2000.

Mortimore, P., P. Sammons, L. Stoll, D. Lewis, R. Ecob, *School Matters: The Junior Years.* London: Open Books, 1988.

Newmann, Fred M. and Gary G. Wehlage, *Succesful School Restructuring.* Madison, Wisconsin: Center on Organization and Restructuring of Schools, 1995.

Rosenholtz, S. J. *Teachers' Workplace: The Social Organization of Schools.* New York: Longmans, 1989.

Sanders, W.L. and J.C. Rivers, "Cumulative and Residual Effects of Teachers on Future Student Academic Achievement." Knoxville, TN: University of Tennessee Value-Added Research and Assessment Center, 1996.

Saphier, Jonathon. "Bonfires and Magic Bullets." Research for Better Teaching, Carlisle, MA. 1994.

Saphier, Jonathon. *How to Make Supervision and Evaluation Really Work.* Research for Better Teaching, Carlisle, MA. 1993.

Saphier, Jonathon and Matthew King. "Good Seeds Grow Strong Cultures." *Educational Leadership.* March, 1985.

Saphier, Jonathon, Barbara Ascheim, and Susan Freedman. *Beyond Mentoring: Comprehensive Induction Programs: How to Attract, Support and Retain New Teachers.* Newton: Teachers 21, 2001.

Wildman, Terry M. and Jerome A. Niles, "Reflective Teachers: Tensions between Abstrations and Realities." *Journal of Teacher Education*, July-August, 1987.

ESSAY 3

Including Student Results in Teacher Evaluation – A Case Study in Focus on Teaching Expertise

Abstract

In this era of accountability in education, teachers are asked to be accountable for student results as never before. In Montgomery County, MD this accountability appears in the written evaluation of every teacher. This paper describes: (a) how this accountability avoids a reductionist numbers game tied to test scores; and (b) how joint responsibility for student learning has come about through a powerful alliance of union and administrative leaders.

How to Include Student Results in Teacher Evaluation . . . Responsibly

– Jon Saphier, Mark Simon, Jerry Weast

Accountability has been the watchword in the last decade of education reform; but with all the accountability tools that the standards movement has brought, it is not clear that the focus on accountability has improved the quality of teaching and learning. This is unfortunate since the prime variables in improving student results are teacher knowledge and skill. The time has come to make a closer examination of student results a part of everything we do in education, including teacher evaluation. But we must do so in a way that keeps sight of the main point—to improve teaching as the prime vehicle for improving student achievement. Inappropriate assumptions about causation and inappropriate stakes and consequences can make accountability systems largely counterproductive. It's time to pay more attention to the details of how data are used in evaluating performance of teachers and schools to ensure that the tail isn't wagging the dog. We can thus create a focus on student results that enable us to anchor our work on these vital questions:

- what do we want our students to know and be able to do?
- how will we know that they have learned it?
- what will we do if they haven't?
- what will we do when they already know it?

– Rick DuFour

Should teachers be accountable for student results? Our answer is yes. How then can this accountability be structured to provide for the wide range of differences students bring to a teacher's classroom—differences in prior knowledge, differences in proficiency at reading and writing, differences in the value their family puts on school learning, differences in motivation, differences in health and living conditions that put some children at severe disadvantage for learning in school? How can teachers be held accountable for results when there are so many variables besides their teaching influencing what students learn in a given year?

We have no choice as individual teachers and as a profession but to stand up to our responsibility for taking students from wherever they are when we get them and moving them forward. Further, we have a responsibility to bring all our students to proficiency with literacy and numeracy, even if it takes some longer than others. We cannot be held responsible for the disadvantages students endure before and during their time with us, but we can be accountable for believing in their ability and providing rich and challenging learning environments. And by extension, we must be accountable for showing our work gets results.

Individual teacher accountability for student progress does come with the package we advocate—but not in a way that becomes a numbers game or oversimplifies the complex relationship between what teachers do and what standardized tests measure. The snapshot provided on standardized tests doesn't begin to measure the range and depth of learning we expect of children. Our measures of student learning must be sufficiently complex to capture those subtle but ultimately more important habits of mind in students that come from good teaching and quality education. Student achievement scores on annual tests may be highly inaccurate reflections of the quality of a school or the quality of teaching, as we will demonstrate in the sample evaluations to follow.

Standardized test score data must never, in and of its self, constitute a judgment about the quality of teaching. There are just too many variables that impact high or low scores; too many ways to make scores improve like emphasizing test-taking skills or focusing on the kids at the margins of cut-off scores, all of which have little to do with improving the quality of teaching and learning. The problem with a reductionist approach that reifies standardized test scores as a valid measure of teacher quality, is that it does an injustice to the complexity of teaching. There is no substitute for close observation by a skilled, knowledgeable evaluator.

In a responsible teacher evaluation system, data on student results, such as test scores, provoke questions that are the grist for substantive dialogue about the quality of teaching. We look at real student work of all kinds and ask what might be contributing to patterns in results. What are *we* doing or not doing that contributes to these results? What can we try differently? The data fuels the analysis, augments observations, and becomes the subject of dialogue. Judgment is exercised as to which data are most valuable and which data sheds little light. Data are not used as a short cut way around close observation and analysis of teaching.

Our first thesis in this essay will be that student results should be included in the improvement of teaching and teacher evaluation,

but included in a responsible way. Our second thesis is that including student results must serve the larger and more important thrust of developing shared responsibility for student learning across the school system.

The purpose, then, of examining student data is the creation of a schoolhouse culture in which looking at student work and other data about student progress becomes a part of the way we do business. *The process is as much the point as the measurement of results.* Educators in a school must be asking tough questions, trying new strategies together, and engaging in honest self-critique. In short, developing a true professional community in each school and throughout the district is what we are advocating. If properly done, attention to student results can generate processes with broad ownership. Insistence that good teaching must include an analysis of student learning is essential to productive schools and a healthy teaching and learning culture.

In Montgomery County, Maryland, responsible use of student results is the goal of the District with an ongoing partnership, not with opposition from the Montgomery County Education Association (the teachers' union). What makes the inclusion of student results responsible is: (a) defining "results" as far more than standardized test scores, (b) sharing responsibility for student learning through joint union/district design, implementation and evaluation of the professional growth/evaluation system, and (c) maintaining the emphasis on the complexities of improving teaching and learning and avoiding the pitfalls of the numbers game based simply on test scores or performance pay. In this piece, are four examples of what final evaluations look like when student results are included in what we are calling a "responsible" way.

In part I of this paper, we will share these evaluations and expand on what an evaluation system looks like that creates them. In part II, we will focus on what it takes for individuals to produce a school district to support comprehensive, results-driven teacher evaluations like the four in this text.

Part I

What Are "Results?"

A good system of analyzing student results in teacher evaluations would be able to say the following:

1. Student learning is the target, and test results are held as an indicator of it, not the full measure of it. Student results means more than standardized test scores.
2. Student results are used to stimulate courageous conversations among educators about the cause and effect connections between what they are doing and what students are learning.
3. Evaluations are narrative. Student results including numerical scores from standardized tests are only included in the narrative in the light of observational data. The meaning of data is not assumed.
4. Pay raises are never connected to standardized test scores, though this does not rule out a more professional way of recognizing superior performance. (We are in the midst of creating a "career lattice" that will recognize superior teaching as a pre-requisite to pay increases tied to additional responsibilities.)

There are many kinds of results that are important for students beyond what standardized tests measure. Students may show a capacity to analyze and synthesize data, ideas, or competing opinions. This is important in the workplace and important for citizenship as well. They may demonstrate their capacity to do these things in their writing, in their projects, and in their verbal presentations. Standardized tests in a given state may not assess these capacities; but a skillful teacher will have these learnings as targets and have data about student progress on these learnings. A good evaluator will have gathered data on targets like these and be able to document student progress.

An additional important result is the teaching of students to work together in an effective way to get something meaningful done. The SCANS report of the U.S. Department of Labor (1992) cited the ability to work productively in groups as one of the most important demands of the 21st century workplace. The same finding is echoed in the summary of workplace demands in Murnane and Levy's *The New Basic Skills* (1996).

The results that concern Americans most these days, however, are that too many of our public school graduates, especially our city kids, have inadequate literacy and numeracy skills. These are concrete and measurable results our country has a right to expect from its public schools. Unfortunately, our society does not sufficiently support teaching staffs, especially in its cities, for teachers to provide the quality of education they could. We have the knowledge; we even have loads of motivated young adults willing to undertake the job. But we do not have the staff development support, the working conditions, the demanding knowledge-based certification requirements, or the job incentives to attract and keep able teachers in our toughest schools. Provisions for certification in the new ESEA law will help, but there is no provision in the new law to support continuous teacher learning or to raise teacher salaries to attract young people to earn the certification. So the argument can plausibly be made that, along with accountability for student results, must come support for getting the job done. We are strong supporters of this argument. In fact, it has been the premise of teacher accountability in Montgomery County that teachers must have adequate resources, schools must have adequate staffing, and the teacher corps must have supportive working conditions if teachers are to be accountable for student results. We are fortunate to have a community and a school board that have strived to provide these things; and we are willing to be held accountable for student results in return. Anything less would be unprofessional on our part.

So let us now look at this concept of "results" and how a fair reporting system might be constructed that connects teacher performance to meaningful student results.

The Relation of Teaching to "Results"

Paradoxically, it is possible for students to be doing well on standardized tests while receiving poor teaching. One can conjure many reasons this could be so (e.g., highly motivated kids who come well prepared to a high school AP teacher). These students do the work themselves while the teacher sits back and expects the students to complete their assignments and get ready for the AP test. The few kids who struggle get little help, are made to feel inadequate, and may slip through the cracks. Yet, the overall test scores make the teacher look good. We include an evaluation of such a teacher in the section that follows. Despite good student scores, this person's teaching is so inadequate that he receives an overall "unsatisfactory" rating and is put into the Peer Assistance and Review (PAR) process. His job is at risk if he doesn't improve.

It is also possible for a teacher to be doing an outstanding job and be producing significant student results, just not the kind of results that show up yet on standardized tests. Take, for example, a first grade teacher whose students arrive not knowing the alphabet, have barely any phonemic awareness, and most can't sit still for more than one minute at classroom meeting. By the end of the winter, these children have learned how to function in school, complete tasks, can be attentive for a 20 minute meeting, and most know the alphabet. They understand the conventions of writing as recorded talk and have done "interactive writing" for their first print messages. They still can't budge the needle much on the Metropolitan test, but this teacher will be passing along a group of youngsters ready, as well as eager to learn, to the second grade teacher. Even though her standardized test scores haven't moved much, documentation of student results of a different kind shows the reader that this teacher has done an outstanding job. A complete final evaluation write up of this kind of teacher is included also in the section that follows.

Considering quality of teaching and correspondent standardized test scores, there are four possibilities represented in the following graphic (see figure 1).

Figure 1

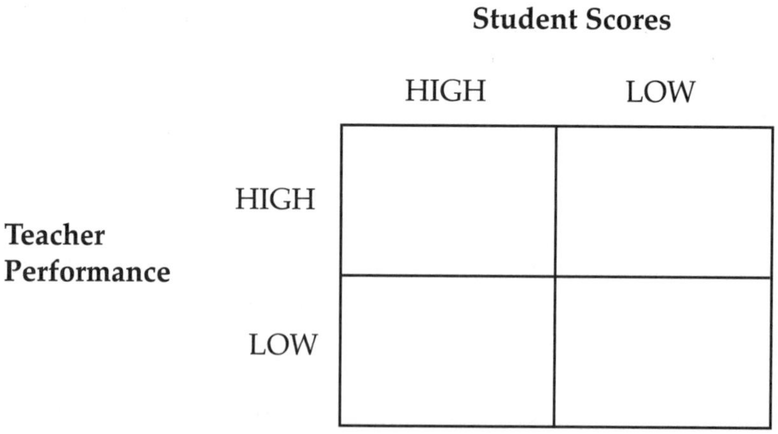

		Student Scores	
		HIGH	LOW
Teacher Performance	HIGH		
	LOW		

One can be practicing: (1) high quality teaching and getting good standardized test scores, (2) unsatisfactory teaching and have good scores, (3) unsatisfactory teaching and poor scores, and (4) high quality teaching and poor scores. With good analysis and documenting skills, an evaluator can show credible and convincing evidence of all four cases. We have included examples of all four below. Notice that the evidence of what the teacher has done and what results have been produced for students are included in narrative report form. Numbers certainly have a place. Standardized test scores also have a place. But the central questions are always: what kind of student progress has been achieved; how much; and how much of it can be attributed to the teacher's work? And standardized tests, though included, are far from the only measure of the outcomes of teaching.

Here are four samples of final evaluation summaries of a teacher's performance. See if you can tell which write-up represents which box of the matrix in figure 1 as you read.

Data about student results are highlighted by bold print in the text.

Note:
The reader may think the evaluations to follow are long and require much time and effort. While we do written evaluations for any teacher in any year if there are concerns about the teacher's performance, the normal cycle calls for these comprehensive written reviews only once every five years. Thus, evaluators are not swamped in paper work. In the years between formal written evaluations, administrators must continue to visit classes and dialog with teachers, but there are no written demands for lengthy documentation of the visits. Teachers, however, must engage in rigorous, substantive self-development plans each year in which they are reviewed. Readers more interested in policy implications of this essay may want to return later to the evaluation samples that follow, and skip to Part II on page 138.

Sample Evaluations

Final Evaluation Summary

Teacher: **Jim Turner** **Date:** 5/25/02

Subject/Grade: **7, 8 Mathematics** **School:** Osgood

Evaluator: **Evangeline Clark**

The evaluator will summarize, in narrative form, the teacher's performance on the following standards (use additional sheets of paper as necessary).

I. Teachers are committed to students and their learning.

II. Teachers know the subjects they teach and how to teach those subjects to students.

III. Teachers are responsible for establishing and managing student learning in a positive learning environment.

IV. Teachers continually assess student progress, analyze the results and adapt instruction to improve student achievement.

V. Teachers are committed to continuous improvement and professional development.

VI. Teachers exhibit a high degree of professionalism.

Performance Standard I. Teachers are committed to students and their learning.

- Mr. Turner's response pattern challenges the quick student but does not lower standards for those who need more time to grasp material. He routinely uses wait time and cues and perseveres with students to stimulate their thinking, as well as to build confidence. (see 10/9 and 11/6/97) During the last ten minutes of class (see 10/9/97, 2/5/98), he often pulls together small groups of students who are confused and reteaches the material in a different way while other students work in pairs on similar challenge problems.

- Mr. Turner's portfolio has logs of monthly meetings with other 8th grade math teachers in his building from 1996-99. His records include notes on case studies of individual students' difficulties , suggestions for alternative approaches he got from his colleagues, students' grades, and work samples showing what happened to performance after strategies were tried. During our conference, Mr. Turner pointed out the impact that manipulative materials had had on **CRT results for 8 different individuals; gain scores ranged from 35 to 85 points. He also noted improvements in overall performance on problem-solving that occurred after the 8th grade team began to use computer tutorials to supplement extra help sessions (see conference notes of 2/5.)**

- Mr. Turner both preaches continuous improvement and sets up policies and practices which make that belief come alive. Assignments must be handed in on time and represent the student's best effort to meet the criteria for success. After feedback, students have an opportunity to re-do certain assignments or to take on an added challenge within specified time limits. Students who really want to apply themselves, try hard problems, ask for help, and work strategically, get their highest earned grade for an assignment. Thus, he confirms the value of pushing oneself to improve performance. (see conference notes re: grading and incentives, 9/13; see also project criteria sheets and samples of students "re-dos")

- Knowing the importance of including students' own experiences and culture in his curriculum, Mr. Turner has classes demonstrate their understanding of algebraic concepts by assigning them to make up word problems about situations in their neighborhoods that embed the concepts. These have provided humor, motivation, and a way to recognize and use the diverse backgrounds of the learners.

Performance Standard II. Teachers know the subjects they teach and how to teach those subjects to students.

- Mr. Turner uses a variety of methods to help his students master mathematical concepts:
  a) short lectures and demonstrations with immediate application (see 10/7 and 11/6),
  b) frequent use of diagrams and physical models to illustrate mathematical concepts (conference notes, 2/13)
  c) frequent checking procedures (see 10/7 and 11/6)

d) Slavin's STAD model for practicing problem sets and reviewing for the weekly quiz each student takes individually.

Note: ***His grade book shows a sharp drop in failure rate since STAD's introduction.*** *Using research findings about what makes a difference in academic achievement, Mr. Turner is working on teaching students to analyze their strategies and group processes to identify areas for improvement after each class.*

- Students in Mr. Turner's classes have wide access both to him and to technology for extra help. All know how to use graphing calculators. He varies using the calculator as a checking and as an instructional device (see 10/9/97, 2/5/98) and also uses supplementary computer tutorial programs for individuals who need another approach to concepts.

- Mr. Turner is a frequent contributor to the work of the mathematics curriculum committee and serves as a math mentor for accelerated students. He was selected to highlight and explain critical 7th grade concepts to parents four times over the last three years. Students routinely describe him as an "excellent explainer."

Performance Standard III. Teachers are responsible for establishing and managing student learning in a positive learning environment.

- Mr. Turner creates a climate of openness and respect through classroom routines such as his "question pass-off and listener summary," his before-class thinker's challenge, and his notetaker's summary (see 10/9/97, 2/5/98). He greets students one by one at the door and often stands there as they leave to remind them of goals, issue praise for effort or give a bit of encouragement.

- Mr. Turner makes a regular practice of calling each family once in the first month of school to establish contact and express his interest in the child's academic progress. Accomplishing this early communication and sharing something positive before conferences in the fall, he says, lays a solid foundation for honest talk should the student have problems later on. The parents already know he is on their side and difficult conferences are less defensive. Both parent and student surveys show satisfaction. "He's really tough on us, but I know he cares," is a comment from one student oft repeated by others in similar language.

- Students share responsibility for their class's success. Each class rotates the job of taking notes for absentees who are then responsible for checking the notes folder as soon as they return. In order to insure accountability and emphasize good summarizing, Mr. Turner has the note-taker explain the notes to him at the end of class; other students can then contribute missing pieces.

- Mr. Turner is proficient both at structuring cooperative groups and at letting students select a variety of ways to work together or alone. While he has required all his students to learn the social skills of cooperative work (listening, checking others' understanding), he also respects their individual styles and provides room for them to use their strengths.

Performance Standard IV. Teachers continually assess student progress, analyze results, and adapt instruction to improve student achievement.

- Weekly lesson plans routinely included two or more assessment activities that allowed Mr. Turner to gather data about student progress; students used learning logs three or more times a week and were given detailed feedback on how well they were doing at meeting the grade level standards; Mr. Turner also instituted a monthly "strategy" session during which he shared his analysis of what each student needed to do to improve, identified "key strategies" that would make a difference, and asked students to set goals for themselves. (see folder entries from 10/7/98, 1/12/99, 2/13/99)

- During conferences after both announced and unannounced visits, Mr. Turner clearly explained how he used data from both MSPAP and Criterion Referenced Testing to make decisions about emphasis in a unit; in several instances, conclusions drawn from data (e.g., a pattern of poor performance on problems involving statistics and probability) caused him to seek additional support materials and to design new activities for required units. In each observation session, I noted the use of a "diagnostic" assessment activity.

- The student work that was displayed throughout the year and that we reviewed during our conferences consistently demonstrated an emphasis on using data about performance to improve the next attempt **at meeting the standards.** Several displays included multiple drafts in which students had done significant revisions, explanatory paragraphs in which students (a) analyzed what they had not understood initially and (b) explained how they had used what they learned during subsequent class sessions to improve their next attempt. (see samples in folder)

- **Analysis of CRT scores for this year and the past three years shows** a consistent pattern of gain scores above the county average for Mr. Turner's students. **He is particularly effective with** children of color where 75% are at grade level or above . Eight of his incoming 7th graders had math achievement which the grade level team deemed "at risk" of not making it into an 8th grade algebra section. Six of these students (including all three children of color) ended the year at or near grade level and were assigned to the algebra section for 8th grade math.

Performance Standard V. Teachers are committed to continuous improvement and professional development.

- Mr. Turner collects anonymous surveys from his students each year asking for feedback on his teaching. When feedback indicated problems with the timing of complex homework assignments, he was able to work with other teachers on his team to organize a more reasonable load for students yet not sacrifice the standards and rigor he wanted.

- Two years ago, Mr. Turner started a monthly math department study group. Colleagues bring articles and techniques for teaching particular concepts they have come across in their reading. These sessions often focus on particular students and how new strategies can be brought to their instruction. Mr. Turner regularly brings up his students for review in these sessions.

- As one of his 1997-98 goals, Mr. Turner focused on student goal-setting and self assessment, both of which are associated with higher long-term achievement. Mr. Turner observed two colleagues from Redlands' exemplary goal-setting project, met with the Mathematics Coordinator, and had several colleagues observe him and collect data. His plan and end-of-year report were tightly designed and showed he had learned and applied a variety of strategies (see folder samples).

Performance Standard VI. Teachers exhibit a high degree of professionalism.

- Mr. Turner participates actively in all department and faculty meetings and was a key contributor to the building SES plan. He is punctual and responsible in fulfilling hallway and other duties.

- He played a leadership role in developing the school homework policy and involving parents in the process through evening forums. Minutes of the meetings show he personally pressed for high standards and meaningful work, and devised with his department colleagues a system for checking on homework that gives student prompt feedback. This policy has been implemented across the math department.

Summary

Mr. Turner combines a strong belief in students with a wide range of teaching skills. He draws alternatives from his large repertoire when students are not responding, and is persistent and personable in sending high expectation messages to all students. He achieves strong productivity and does so with students from all backgrounds and of different learning styles. His importance to the staff is augmented by his strong contributions to the whole school community.

Meets or exceeds standards of Montgomery County Public Schools (X)

Below standards of Montgomery County Public Schools ( )

Evaluator ____________________________________ Date _______

Teacher ____________________________________ Date _______

Teacher's signature below indicates he/she has read the report. Signature does not necessarily indicate agreement with the report.

....

As is probably clear to the reader, Jim Turner is a skilled teacher who is getting good results. Notice how data easily fits in narrative text, yet is precise and quantifiable where appropriate. Some data are about gain scores on Criterion Referenced Tests; some are about decrease in failure rate; some are evidence that students can use feedback to make significant improvements in writing drafts; and finally, there is an analysis of the achievement of children of color.

The next Summary Evaluation document is of Virginia Hyskill, whose first grade class, at the end of the year, cannot produce very impressive results on standardized literacy tests.

Final Evaluation Summary

Teacher: **Virginia Hyskil** Date: **5/25/02**

Subject/Grade: **2nd Grade** School: **Dupuis**

Evaluator: **Carol Insight**

The evaluator will summarize, in narrative form, the teacher's performance on the following standards (use additional sheets of paper as necessary).

I. Teachers are committed to students and their learning.

II. Teachers know the subjects they teach and how to teach those subjects to students.

III. Teachers are responsible for establishing and managing student learning in a positive learning environment.

IV. Teachers continually assess student progress, analyze the results and adapt instruction to improve student achievement.

V. Teachers are committed to continuous improvement and professional development.

VI. Teachers exhibit a high degree of professionalism.

Performance Standard I. Teachers are committed to students and their learning.

- Ms. Hyskil has demonstrated her belief that virtually all students can learn although she has faced numerous challenges this year. Only two of her 24 students had attained first grade reading level at the start of second grade. Many students' attendance was erratic; three youngsters were pulled from school for three months by their families and then returned in mid-year. In addition, a higher than usual quota of students with ADD and two particularly difficult children made classroom management very complicated in the opening months of school. Despite these obstacles, Ms. Hyskill has worked skillfully and diligently to build a foundation of skills that will position her students for solid academic achievement in years ahead

Her first objectives were to build students' ability to attend, function responsibly and follow the routines of the classroom. Her success here is described under standard III below. Her second set of measurable outcomes focused on the behaviors displayed by competent emerging readers and writers (see Early Literacy Indicators adopted 6/98). In the opening days of school, her children were disorderly, unresponsive to behavioral corrections, unable to follow multi-step directions, unable to engage in print tasks or attend to reading aloud for more than a few minutes. **By May, her class was a model of order and busy engagement with academic tasks.** Their significant progress from non-readers to emerging readers may not have been captured on standardized comprehension tests, but **23 of 24 children were able to work independently on story writing and seven children who had not been able to decode at all in September were able read aloud from a "just right" book which they had chosen themselves.**

- Ms. Hyskil consistently encourages students and provides help in ways that credit their ability to do hard work. Observation notes of 10/19 and 12/6 have numerous examples of critical incidents where she responds sensitively to student frustration with encouragement and specific cues. *("I can't do these. They're too hard." "Well, they are hard. But you've done the first four just right, so I know you've got the brainpower. What part of this one don't you understand?")* She holds students gently but firmly accountable for finishing meaningful tasks, even while granting breaks or switching gears for a while.

- Students get daily feedback on their work and correct all mistakes themselves, either from answer sheets Ms. Hyskil provides or in paired "editing" with other students. Students must explain the reasons for their corrections to Ms. Hyskil before taking their papers home. Being a "good explainer" of your corrections (see 1/17) is highly valued and praised in the class, so being speedy is less important than understanding. She builds confidence by teaching her students that errors are opportunities for learning.

Performance Standard II. Teachers know the subjects they teach and how to teach those subjects to students.

- At the beginning of the year, two students in Ms. Hyskil's class still struggled with phonic awareness of initial consonant sounds, although they had alphabetic recognition. After consulting with the reading specialist , Ms. Hyskil adopted a set of strategies specifically targeted to help these students make progress toward meeting grade level standards. She also provided a set of materials for parents to use at home. While they were working to catch up on their skill deficiencies, both children were full and active members of literature discussions and were able to participate in "reading" predictable texts and class poems. **Both youngsters can now do beginning decoding, and comprehend stories read to them at a high second grade level. They can read books at the "D" level in guided reading.**

- All students spend at least a half-hour daily in book groups with Ms. Hyskil or her aide. In addition, the total class meets as a group daily to play language games (see observation of 9/23 when children holding word cards arranged themselves to make sensible sentences in various ways). She has diagnosed the perceptual strengths and learning styles of all her students and varies her reading instruction accordingly (assessment instruments student profiles shared at conference of 10/19). Her astounding repertoire of materials and approaches, always focused on specific learning outcomes, has resulted in consistent high engagement of **her students and steady progress as demonstrated in her reading records and portfolios for each child (see standard IV).**

- Ms. Hyskil has a created a collection of cassette tapes that use a strategy for slow reading and chunking by units of meaning. She constantly adds books her individual students want to learn to read and has them read aloud between the pauses in her taped phrases. As a result of practicing at this slow pace with her voice and the visual cues of the page, over a dozen of her children can actually read these short books.

- A master of using manipulative materials to illustrate mathematical ideas, Ms. Hyskil always has students verbalize in full sentences what they are doing when they, for example, trade 10 white rods for an orange. (From observation of 12/6.)

Performance Standard III. Teachers are responsible for establishing and managing student learning in a positive learning environment.

- Early in the year, many students were unable to sit still for over two minutes without fidgeting or disrupting in some way. This behavior was also present in small instructional groups. **By Thanksgiving, Ms. Hyskil could hold 10-minute meetings with good focus from the whole class including three children who had been diagnosed with ADD.** She worked very effectively during the first two weeks of school to teach routines and establish patterns of respect among students. Observations of 9/23 and 10/19 show evidence of her constant vigilance, high standards, and positive attribution in her corrective moves to refocus students ("Tony, you forgot that we were listening to Jamey. I know you can be a good listener.")

- Students know they are safe and will be treated fairly when conflicts arise. The **number of fights between students in Ms. Hyskil's class in the cafeteria, hallway, and play yard has decreased from several a day to one or less a week.** She has used immediate interventions and a special time out procedure to end conflicts swiftly. More importantly, she has gone on to teach her students conflict resolution strategies , an approach which is unprecedented in the school. Students now generate alternatives for handling situations of conflict and practice restitution for wrongs to others (see dialogs from 12/6 observation).

- Every night since the second week of school, Ms. Hyskil has called two families of children in her class to share good news and get to know parents and their concerns. She has used a personalized library of short books to send home with children for parents to read to them and has had great success in using these experiences to engage both parents and children in conversations. Several other teachers have adopted the practice.

- Ms. Hyskil's 24 second graders, most non-readers, have a history of erratic attendance through grade K and 1. Until this year, seven families had never had a representative at a parent conference or back to school night. Largely as a result of Ms Hyskil's efforts, **all but one family has attended at least one school function this year** and all families have responded more positively to contact with school personnel than in the past.

Performance Standard IV. Teachers continually assess student progress, analyze results, and adapt instruction to improve student achievement.

- In addition to daily language and writing groups, Ms. Hyskil meets weekly with each child individually to do assessment and goal setting for reading and writing skills. She has up to date "running reading records" with details of each child's decoding ability and attainments in developmental skills (using context clues, word recognition, punctuation, etc.). Individual tasks are constructed for each child congruent with their goals. A parent volunteer corps of 8 people she has recruited from the school community works individually with the youngsters who most need extra tutoring to meet their goals. Ms. Hyskil prepares packets for each of these volunteers weekly and has a monthly group supervision session on Friday afternoons. This is an extraordinary commitment to providing individualized instruction and supervised practice for her students.

- **Average engaged time per student has increased from <40% to >75%.** Ms.Hyskil's data comes from time study records she asked her colleague, Ms. Donahue, to collect during several peer observations this year and is confirmed by her evaluator's tallies as well. Logs, checklists and running records from the Reading Initiative data forms show that **over 65% of Ms. Hyskil's students have exceeded one grade level of growth on literacy indicators. Seven of her students can now read independently at the first grade level,** a huge increase from their incoming proficiency.

- While few of her students are on grade level in math, **her class logs of mastery of MCPS objectives show significant progress** for most of her students. She arranged tutoring by 5th graders for several of her students who lagged furthest behind. Though their progress remained slow, by the end of the year, they were looking forward to working with their "big brother" and "big sister" tutors after previously rejecting working on math at all. Ms. Hyskil has consulted with the area math specialist and varied the materials used with these students to match their visual and tactile learning styles.

- Ms. Hyskill has constructed a bar graph with data on each student to analyze progress on Reading Initiative checklists by race. The top three scoring students, including the two students reading at grade level, are white. These results are appropriate, given entry skills of her students.

Performance Standard V. Teachers are committed to continuous improvement and professional development.

- Ms. Hyskil has both consulted and led her colleagues at weekly grade level meetings, in examining new strategies to involve students in authentic experiences, and then writing in their journals about these experiences. She attended a course in primary literacy with special emphasis on spelling and grammar to try to bring to her team perspective on this issue for emerging readers and writers. As a result, she and her colleagues have developed an easily accessed "spelling bank" for commonly used words in her class. Students who are ready, use this tool after they have produced written products. Several of her students are still at the stage of dictating stories to her and to volunteers and are not ready for this device yet.

Performance Standard VI. Teachers exhibit a high degree of professionalism.

- Ms. Hyskil participates actively in faculty meetings. She has become an informal second mentor for a new teacher. The teacher's official mentor is in another building. She has been very generous with her time, especially on Friday afternoons, and checks in with the new teacher to debrief the week and help her look ahead.

- She played a leadership role in the development of the new playground policy and the development of peer mediation training — an integral part of the playground policy. She attended the training herself and has been an effective coach to the upper grade children who are implementing the mediation strategies.

Summary

Ms. Hyskil has done a marvelous job of building a smooth flowing and warm environment where children are active and learning all day long. She is to be commended for her extraordinary accomplishments in moving all children forward. A large number of children entering with behavioral and academic profiles that put them at risk for school failure are now ready to learn. Next year's teacher will inherit a class willing and able to advance from a strong foundation in literacy and numeracy.

Meets or exceeds standards of Montgomery County Public Schools (X)

Below standards of Montgomery County Public Schools ( )

Evaluator ________________________________ Date ________

Teacher ________________________________ Date ________

Teacher's signature below indicates he/she has read the report. Signature does not necessarily indicate agreement with the report.

....

By the end of the year, Ms. Hyskil's children cannot budge the score very much on the Metropolitan test, which the district uses to assess literacy progress. But clearly, she has brought them a long way — and the data supports that conclusion. The data, however, that allows us to see how much she has achieved is not from standardized tests. From "disorderly and unresponsive," her students have become a model of order and busy engagement with academic tasks, able to work independently and sit attentively at classroom meetings. Fights are down, engagement is up (both quantifiable indicators). But most important, running records, class logs, checklists, and records of books read, show that 65% of her students have gained more than one year in readiness indicators. So in sum, standardized test scores may still be low, but a range of data shows that her teaching is achieving excellent results on other measures of academic progress.

The details of the narrative write-up tells us much about why she is getting these results. Excellent feedback on student work, classroom climate building, confidence building all take place and evidence tell us how she does these things. Thus, we have a skilled teacher whose skills are supported by evidence and whose results are documented in credible and convincing ways.

....

Our next teacher, Ms. Marsh is not doing too well.

Final Evaluation Summary

Teacher: **Sybil Marsh** Date: **5/25/02**

Subject/Grade: **7, 8 Mathematics** School: **Osgood**

Evaluator: **Arthur Clark**

The evaluator will summarize, in narrative form, the teacher's performance on the following standards (use additional sheets of paper as necessary).

I. Teachers are committed to students and their learning.

II. Teachers know the subjects they teach and how to teach those subjects to students.

III. Teachers are responsible for establishing and managing student learning in a positive learning environment.

IV. Teachers continually assess student progress, analyze the results and adapt instruction to improve student achievement.

V. Teachers are committed to continuous improvement and professional development.

VI. Teachers exhibit a high degree of professionalism.

Performance Standard I. Teachers are committed to students and their learning.

- Ms. Marsh's pattern of communicating expectations and structuring instruction is not designed to help all students in the classroom learn and achieve at high levels. During 3 separate announced observations (10/15/98, 11/30/98, 3/18/99) Ms. Marsh went through the same process of reviewing homework problems one by one. She called only on students who raised their hands, to assist her in solutions for board problems. Three or four individuals, all male, did most of the responding. The majority of the class were neither called upon nor checked to see if they were following her explanations.

On both 10/15 and 11/30, I observed several students copying problems off the board, which suggested they had not done the homework. Questioned about those students in the post conferences, Ms. Marsh remarked that the class was "above some of the students' heads" and that she knew precisely who they were. She said at least by letting them have something to hand in they could hold on to a bit of self-esteem. She rejected my suggestion that self-esteem comes through achievement and mastery and that she was not doing them a favor by allowing them to slide through. When asked how they performed on quizzes and exams, she replied, "they fail most of them." When asked what supplementary instruction she arranged for these students, she replied, "It's really not much use when I have so many other motivated kids who need my help." When asked (10/15/98) why she gives these students tests she knows they will fail instead of using test time for some remedial instruction, she said she hadn't thought of it, but it might be a good idea. At the April conference, she said she had not had time to try that strategy yet.

- I observed no examples of varying instruction for different learning styles or for students with rich but different cultural backgrounds. When asked how she provides for such differences, Ms. Marsh replied that the daily extra help time she provides after school is when she individualizes.

- Ms. Marsh is consistently available in her classroom after 8th period. On several drop-in visits, I noted that sometimes she was alone and sometimes one or two students were working with her. These were students from the top third of the class working with her for help on extra credit problems. I asked if any of the low performing students ever showed up. She said, "rarely." When I suggested she make appointments with the ones she felt needed the most help, she replied, "I feel they have to take responsibility for their own learning. Isn't that one of the goals of our school?"

- Ms. Marsh's lack of pursuit of low performing students together with the minimal interaction she has with them in class is sending consistent low expectation messages to a substantial segment of her students. Their confidence needs to be boosted through contact, help, encouragement, and concrete skill building. This is not happening at an acceptable level.

Performance Standard II. Teachers know the subjects they teach and how to teach those subjects to students.

- All classes observed were recitation lessons involving teacher generated recall questions and student answers. The objective was expressed as "covering" Chapter X or the material that had been assigned. These periods were followed by teacher lecture / presentation on the board, followed by having individual students practice for about ten minutes until the end of class. No group work or manipulatives were observed. Ms. Marsh missed the opportunity to have students work in pairs and help each other. She circulated once around the class during the last five minutes; other than that time, she waited at her desk for the bell. There was neither a teacher led nor student generated summary.

- After the 10/15 observation, I suggested connecting the algebra to real life situations and using some of the MSPAP sample problems which students generally find complex and engaging. Ms. Marsh "doubted they would benefit from that." I recommended having the students make up word problems that would employ the single variables she was working with. She agreed to try the idea. Later that month she reported to me that "it had been beyond most of them." When I asked to see samples of what they had produced, she said she had discarded them.

- Instruction relies entirely on paper and pencil practice and the use of the chalkboard. During four different drop-in visits and three announced observations, I noted no use of technology, concrete models, visuals or demonstrations using manipulatives, or of the supplementary problem packet prepared by the 8th grade team. In all except one instance, computers in the back of the room were dusty and disconnected. Ms. Marsh admits that she has not yet included technology in her course designs or supplemental work with students. She intends to make it a focus for her professional development next year.

- The lack of both variety in instructional methods and relevance to students' lives, makes Ms. Marsh's instruction boring and deprives students of the alternate ways to think about and master concepts which are available to their classmates in other sections. The lack of opportunities to talk through their thinking in pairs, pose questions, find extensions or work with complex messy problems means students currently performing in the middle and lower third of the class are less likely to be successful on state and district assessment tasks and may be limited from taking higher level courses.

Performance Standard III. Teachers are responsible for establishing and managing student learning in a positive learning environment.

- Ms. Marsh has surprisingly few overt discipline problems. "She'll kill us if we're out of line," said one sophomore to a question of mine after class. Yet she tolerates a high degree of low level talking and off task behavior. This is documented in all three observations conducted this year. Student scans at five minute intervals revealed **over 50% off task time for two thirds of the students. This is unacceptable.**

- There is no evidence of varying formats for individual or small group work. Queried about the persistence of recitation lessons, Ms. Marsh said the format was the best choice for maintaining control and keeping the class on task. Data(cited above)collected from observation does not support this assertion. Ms. Marsh initially claimed that I had come on a bad day. When confronted with the fact that the figures were consistent for all three observations, she replied, "I don't think you can tell all that much from kids' body language."

- Neither observations nor examinations of student work and teacher feedback yielded evidence that Ms. Marsh works on student goal setting and risk taking. Ms. Marsh's response pattern has been documented under standard I. Feedback on student work contains no specific comments about what to improve, and no correction or "see me" messages. I neither observed nor heard accounts of supplemental instruction or persistence with students who struggle. Students who asked for help were treated differently, depending upon whether Ms. Marsh perceived them to be "bright" or not. (see 3/18/99)

Performance Standard IV. Teachers continually assess student progress, analyze results, and adapt instruction to improve student achievement.

- Four different reviews of lesson and unit plans during the school year yielded no evidence that Ms. Marsh knew and was attempting to develop the competencies being assessed either as part of the MCPS CRT program or as part of MSPAP. Three of these lesson plan reviews (12/2/97, 3/19/98, 4/2/98) occurred.

a) after Ms. Marsh had indicated that she did not understand how she was to "use all this test stuff"(10/16/97) and had subsequently been given 2 months of planning support from her Instructional Resource Teacher and
b) after both the principal and the mathematics curriculum specialist had met with Ms. Marsh for a total of 6 hours each to help her practice analyzing student work and planning a variety of ways to reteach concepts which children found troubling.

Thus, while students in other classes were able to work on developing background knowledge and experiences necessary for their future understanding of Algebra, Ms. Marsh's students received little or no opportunity to do so.

- At her request, Ms. Marsh was given copies of the appropriate curriculum guidelines and grade level standards on three different occasions between August 1997 and March 1999. When we conferenced on 4/2/99, however, Ms. Marsh was unable to find any one of the copies. Thus, she was unable to respond to questions about what progress students in her class *should* have made by early April and what next steps they would need to take in order to be ready to demonstrate what they knew.

- At each pre-conference, Ms. Marsh was asked to be prepared to show: (a) how she used informal diagnostic assessments to get data about individual and group performance, and (b) how she used that data to modify instruction. In three of the four classroom observations (10/15/98, 11/30/98, and 3/18/99) Ms. Marsh responded to this request by distributing worksheets and a game, both of which were yellowed and at least 7 years old; in a 4th session she had students engage in the practice of skills not assigned to her grade level and told them that "my diagnosis is that you all disappointed me. I was sure you were smarter than this work shows." Student responses to the computer challenge exercises used during the observation of 3/18/99 and to the requirement that they work in groups to solve problems indicated that they were unfamiliar with both tasks. (see 3/18/99 and 4/11/98).

- **On informal pre-testing conducted by the eighth grade teams in November 1998 and again in January 1999, Ms. Marsh's students were significantly less able to deal with geometry questions.** Ms. Marsh explained that the results were not surprising because she "had not had time to do any geometry yet." When she was asked to examine four years of comparative data showing that her classes had consistently lower performance on geometry items and on open-ended questions requiring application of geometry concepts, Ms. Marsh said that she did not like geometry and probably had skipped many of the activities in the geometry strand because she "thought the kids would get that later."

- Ms. Marsh's CRT scores over the last three years show an average of **70% of her students on grade level by the end of the year, slightly below the school average. When the data are further disaggregated, her low performing students show negative gain scores from the previous year while her average performing students show flat scores.** While many students appear to come to her class motivated and able to do grade level work, students who cannot do the work will fall further behind their age mates. When she was asked whether she knew about the pattern of poor performance and had made any attempt to change her instruction, Ms. Marsh said that "There is not much I can do when the kids come into 7th grade with such weak arithmetic skills and I have to review their number facts over and over again. At no point during a 45 minute discussion of how patterns revealed by test data could be helpful, did Ms. Marsh offer a suggestion about what she might think about or do differently.

Performance Standard V. Teachers are committed to continuous improvement and professional development.

- Ms. Marsh distributed student surveys in January but reported that not all the students returned them to her. Thus, she had no analysis of student feedback to share with me. I asked why she did not have the students fill the surveys out in class to ensure a 100% return rate. She said she did "not want to use class time for such business." I directed her to redo the surveys in the spring. When asked for her analysis in April, she replied that there had been no useful information in the student responses. I find Ms. Marsh's discounting of the usefulness of student input a significant problem.

- Her portfolio documents attendance at a professional development course last year in the use of the graphing calculator. Her end of year report cites introduction of the calculator to her high level algebra class, but not her basic level class where MCPS's own research shows it contributes most to student gain scores. When confronted with this information, Ms. Marsh said her students were not ready for the graphing calculator, since they still had basic algebraic algorithms to master. Denying students access to the visual modeling and rapid processing of graphing calculators, walls low performing pupils off from a significant learning aid. It is both a serious instructional mistake and reveals a lack of belief that all students can improve their performance incrementally given effective effort and strategies.

- Ms. Marsh has attended department and school faculty meetings during which SES plans were made and assessed. She makes substantive contributions to the discussions when the topic is programs for gifted and talented students or teacher professional development.

Performance Standard VI. Teachers exhibit a high degree of professionalism.

- Ms. Marsh performs expected hall duties and files reports and attendance sheets in a timely manner.

Summary

Ms. Marsh's overall performance is not meeting the needs of all students. I find her response to suggestions and direction for improvement unsatisfactory. I therefore recommend her for entrance into the PAR program and intensive assistance throughout next year.

Meets or exceeds standards of Montgomery County Public Schools ( )

Below standards of Montgomery County Public Schools (X)

Evaluator ______________________ Date ________

Teacher ______________________ Date ________

Teacher's signature below indicates he/she has read the report. Signature does not necessarily indicate agreement with the report.

....

There is ample documentation is this evaluation of Ms. Marsh's poor teaching practices. She shows inertia and flat resistance to pursue low performing students or make instruction more relevant. There is no variety in the instruction and poor alignment between her lessons and the curriculum. Finally, the student data reported in Standard IV clinches the unsatisfactory rating. This one, and evaluations like it, are not pleasant to write, but they are at least clear. Poor teaching, poor results.

Now let us look at a report that would not be written under most evaluations systems, because the students appear on the surface to be doing well. But when evaluators have the skills to do detailed analysis of both teaching practice and student results, new doors open.

....

Final Evaluation Summary

Teacher: **Dale Sufferin** Date: **5/25/02**

Subject/Grade: **AP American and European Lit.**

School: **Horace Mann H.S.**

Evaluator: **Geraldine Duffy**

The evaluator will summarize, in narrative form, the teacher's performance on the following standards (use additional sheets of paper as necessary).

I. Teachers are committed to students and their learning.

II. Teachers know the subjects they teach and how to teach those subjects to students.

III. Teachers are responsible for establishing and managing student learning in a positive learning environment.

IV. Teachers continually assess student progress, analyze the results and adapt instruction to improve student achievement.

V. Teachers are committed to continuous improvement and professional development.

VI. Teachers exhibit a high degree of professionalism.

Performance Standard I. Teachers are committed to students and their learning.

- Mr. Sufferin's actions do not consistently help students meet quantifiable learning outcomes. Mr. Sufferin believes that he has high standards for student performance, both in class and on tests and papers. It is difficult, however, for students to know what those standards are. Feedback on work is non-specific and gives students little or no insight on what they have done to earn the judgments. "Very good analysis," "Yes," "No," "Poor" are typical marginal and final comments on papers. I examined an entire set of papers Mr. Sufferin was preparing to return during our preconference on 11/18 and found no variation from this pattern of feedback. When asked about the lack of specificity, Mr. Sufferin said the students knew his expectations because he had "gone over them verbally in September" and that some of them were just lazy. He further said that problems are clarified in class. I saw no such evidence of clarification during my four observations, nor any confirmation from students that they knew what to do to improve. "Well, I guess he just didn't like it." was a typical comment. Students also reported that they rarely took the opportunity to rewrite work because second drafts are simply graded—usually with the same mark as on the first—and never contain comments. Mr. Sufferin needs to devote much more time to giving students specific feedback on how to improve their work and to spend time with them individually explaining this feedback when necessary.

- Few students ask substantive questions in class or elaborate upon or debate one another's responses. During my four observations, three students asked questions at the end of lectures. Two were procedural questions about dates and forms of upcoming tests. One student asked Mr. Sufferin to clarify a point he had made in a lecture about the Great Gatsby. "I don't think we were listening very well this morning, Mr. Smith," was his reply. "I hope your group were taking better notes than you were!" Nine out of twelve students in the honors section said they perceived that Mr. Sufferin regards questions as interruptions or signals of lack of attention and that they go elsewhere to find help when they do not understand something.

- Mr. Sufferin's predominant pattern of teaching, lecture, provides for no student interaction either with the teacher or with other students, and no monitoring mechanisms prior to tests and papers to assess how students are assimilating material. The patterns of teaching illustrated further below show that Mr. Sufferin is committed to presenting his material, but not to students and their learning.

Performance Standard II. Teachers know the subjects they teach and how to teach those subjects to students.

- In my three of my formal observations this fall and winter (see write-ups of 9/20, 10/7,11/18, and 1/6), the pattern of teaching was the same. Mr. Sufferin began the class promptly at the bell with a short lecture on an aspect of the current novel and expected students to take notes. After approximately 20 minutes, he stopped and asked if there were any questions. When I asked later if he ever examines the notes, he replied, "No. They're AP students. That's their responsibility." Following the lecture he divided students into groups of four or five to discuss the material he had presented. No guidelines or questions were provided for these discussions. Mr. Sufferin sat at his desk during this group work, correcting tests. Most students attempted to review their notes with their peers. Some started on the next reading assignment. Mr. Sufferin commented later that cooperative learning groups were encouraged by the county. When I reported the varied quality of discussion I had heard and the confusion of many students, he said he would give some thought to my suggestion for explicit questions and tasks for the groups. I also suggested a time to discuss and a sharing/check-in time at the end of class. He felt my recommendation that he circulate himself and listen to the group conversations would stifle student spontaneity.

- During my 11/18 observation, Mr. Sufferin was reviewing for an upcoming unit test. He asked a series of questions presumably representing essay topics that would appear on the test. He called on seven different students during the class, all white (there are four students of color in this 23 student class). No follow-up or extension questions were asked when the answer he appeared to be seeking was found. When a student failed to give a complete answer, another student was immediately called on to finish. "So what did the train represent in Fitzgerald's imagery?" Student 1 "The charging machine in the garden of American life." Yes, but what else: Tom? (Tom answers.) No student received cues or probes to reveal their thinking. The questions and answers were aimed at producing specific answers Mr. Sufferin had in mind. This kind of dialogue is unacceptable in any class, but especially an AP class where student thinking and analytical skills are as important to develop as their factual knowledge of literature.

Performance Standard III. Teachers are responsible for establishing and managing student learning in a positive learning environment.

- At the beginning of class Mr. Sufferin stands at the door and greets students, often with a joke about their appearance or a personal comment that shows some knowledge of what they're doing in sports or clubs outside of class. There is considerable bantering around his desk before and after class. His good humor is often mentioned in student surveys which, all in all, convey the image of a popular teacher.

- Mr. Sufferin has a reputation in the community as a scholar and a demanding teacher. Many parents ask to have their student assigned to his section, a fact he pointed out to me. Parent surveys confirm that many parents value his toughness. Parents of students in the lower quadrant of his grade distribution, however, are more likely to mention "need for extra help". These comments showed up in various forms in eight surveys I read.

Performance Standard IV. Teachers continually assess student progress, analyze results, and adapt instruction to improve student achievement.

- Students in Mr. Sufferin's classes do well on the AP tests. His percentage of students with 1s and 2s is approximately the same as the rest of the department. The percentage of African-American students scoring 1s and 2s is also about the same as other teachers. The small number of students of color in AP classes at Horace Mann makes statistical comparisons difficult.

- Mr. Sufferin gives grades on unit tests and analytical papers he assigns at the conclusion of novels and poetry units. The grade distribution of As through Cs is approximately a bell curve. Student grades were remarkably consistent over the year, with no examples of low performing students improving and three examples of low performing student scoring lower than in previous years.

- It is difficult to credit the performance of Mr. Sufferin's students on the AP exams, which are near the school average, to his teaching. The students are doing it on their own with very little help from him. There is no evidence of analysis of student results or adaptation or even change in his pattern of instruction to try to elevate the performance of lower performing students. Mr. Sufferin's good personal relationships with students and his reputation for "toughness" allow him to get by without standing out in a school where parental expectations are high and students in his classes are strongly motivated to get help elsewhere. Thus, they continue to do well on AP exams. Mr. Sufferin must take improving student performance seriously and provide the clear expectations, periodic checking, and help to all his students that will raise all boats.

Performance Standard V. Teachers are committed to continuous improvement and professional development.

- This fall, Mr. Suifferin arranged a joint seminar with department members, George Washington University graduate students, and visiting Professor Dimitri Koskiosko from Berkeley on "parallels between modern Russian and American literature". Several department members attended the series and reported it to be an enriching academic experience.

Performance Standard VI. Teachers exhibit a high degree of professionalism.

- Mr. Sufferin participates actively in all department and faculty meetings and was a contributor to the building SES plan. He is punctual and responsible in fulfilling hallway and other duties.

- He has accepted requests to run department meetings when the chair is unavailable and produced minutes for review each time.

Summary

Mr. Sufferin displays an exceedingly narrow range of teaching skills. He has inappropriate expectations of all his students' ability to frame their own questions and absorb material on their own. He does little to cultivate interaction, intellectual dialog, or reflective thinking in his classes. He has been resistant to analyzing student results in relation to his own teaching and rejected suggestions for change. I recommend him for intensive assistance under the PAR program.

Meets or exceeds standards of Montgomery County Public Schools ( )

Below standards of Montgomery County Public Schools (X)

Evaluator ______________________________ Date ________

Teacher ______________________________ Date ________

Teacher's signature below indicates he/she has read the report. Signature does not necessarily indicate agreement with the report.

....

Student results on their own would not have put Mr. Sufferin into the spotlight. His failure rate is not that much higher than others that it would attract the attention of any but the most careful inspectors. His teaching, however, is clearly unsatisfactory on many dimensions; as readers we become convinced of that by the ample documentation. And behind this documentation lie the classroom observations referenced in the text.

What skillful evaluation allows us to do is demand high standards of teaching from all our people...even those who get results they don't deserve. There are signs in the data that Mr. Sufferin's teaching is a cracked edifice, hidden by the motivation his AP students bring to their work despite his insufficient teaching. But when we analyze the teaching in depth, the inadequacy is revealed.

....

Part II

What does it take for individuals to produce and a school district to support, comprehensive and results-driven teacher evaluations like the four above?

Multiple-Year Cycles Designed to Emphasize Professional Growth

Teacher evaluation is part of a multiple-year Professional Growth Cycle in Montgomery. Teacher evaluation is taken seriously, but it is secondary in the design to supporting the Professional Learning Community among the adults in a school and continual improvement of teaching for people who are competent professionals. Don't get us wrong: unsatisfactory teaching is dealt with in ways that are direct and decisive. Intensive assistance is provided for low performing teachers and those who do not improve are dismissed. Approximately 100 teachers a year out of 11,000 have left our teaching force because of poor performance since we initiated our Professional Growth cycle two years ago. But firing bad teachers is not the purpose of the cycle. The purpose is providing resources and structures for the constant improvement of the good people we already have, which as in most districts, is the vast majority of our workforce.

The staffing and supervisory ratios in most American schools make it impossible for administrators to do comprehensive teacher evaluations with thoroughness, quality, and full documentation annually. Class visits and feedback conversations should be on-going, every year, for every teacher. And formal evaluation must be an option for any teacher, any year when there are concerns. But recognize (as all functioning administrators do) that it's the paperwork associated with formal evaluations that is the killer when the supervisory ratio is between 25 to 1 and 50 to 1 (vs. the recognized optimum ratio in industry of between 8 and 12 to 1). Therefore, one purpose of the multiple-year Professional Growth Cycle is to reduce this paper load without reducing the quality and intensity of supervision and feedback teachers receive.

Non-tenured teachers in Montgomery are still evaluated every year for their first three years of employment, but the load is divided between the principal and a corps of Consulting Teachers released from the classroom for three-year tours of duty. Tenured teachers enter a cycle that gradually expands to formal evaluation every five years.

Overall, this structure significantly reduces paper work for evaluators; but we realize we still need to do more on that score.

The Consulting Teachers are part of the union/management collaboratively run Peer Assistance and Review (PAR) program that serves both teachers new to teaching and tenured teachers with below standard evaluations. PAR has proven to provide better intensive support to bring teachers up to standard than our previous system of administrators and school based supports. That allows school based supports to focus on the Professional Growth Cycle for the vast majority of teachers who meet standard.

The main feature of this Professional Growth Cycle is that structures and support have been created that both challenge and enable teachers to be responsible for their own constant improvement. In the years between formal evaluations, teachers are required to undertake self-designed and substantive programs of instructional improvement tailored to their needs and the needs of their students. Ramping things up further, peer visits and analysis of teaching are required for all Montgomery teachers several times during at least one year of the cycle. Staff Development Teachers are available in each building to assist with annual professional growth plans, and to ensure that they are substantive and not fluff.

The creation of the Staff Development Teacher position in every school represents a major commitment of the county to the development of teachers as the key to the improvement of student results. We are convinced that examining the structure of the workplace for teachers and focusing resources on increasing their capacity is central to improving student results. And we don't want readers to be scared off as we profile the steps we have taken to accomplish these new structures in Montgomery County: "Oh, we could never afford that." This effort and these positions come from redistributing and focusing resources where they can do the most good for student learning. Others have done the same by reallocating the resources they already have (District #2 in New York City; Jefferson County Colo.). Equally important is joining the examination of student results to building a strong professional community of openness and non-defensive self-examination of practice. Our Staff Development Teachers are one potent way of focusing on this critical facet of school culture.

It is important to note that these new positions allow much more effective use of administrators' time. Total number of evaluations is reduced through the multiple-year cycle. Consulting teachers reduce the net number of formal observation write-ups the principal must do, yet keeps him/her in the loop. Consulting teachers magnify the administrators' reach to help struggling beginning and experienced teachers. The principal now has able partners in instructional leadership and can focus his/her time where it is most needed in supervision and evaluation and other aspects of instructional leadership.

For other details, write to us for our Professional Growth Cycle Handbook. We recognize that details are important, but we would like in this article to return to the main theme: what does it take to make inclusion of student results in teacher evaluations serve the broader agenda of a data based culture of continuous improvement for student learning? The point we have tried to make here is that it is possible to design a multiple-year Professional Growth Cycle in which teacher evaluation goes on all the time, not just in episodic spasms, and makes it the responsibility of more than just the principal. We can have systems that reduce paperwork, reduce the frequency of formal teacher evaluation, but actually makes the assessment of teaching effectiveness an every year, all-the-time event that includes teacher colleagues and teachers themselves in a professional way.

Demands of Data Gathering – Sources Beyond Classroom Observation

Readers will see from the sample evaluations above, that the data about the teacher's performance came from more than just classroom observations by administrators. The teacher him/herself was a significant source of data, especially for areas pertaining to one's own professional development and relations with the staff, parents and community.

We use a framework for Teaching and Learning to guide our data collection. The six areas about which we collect data are:

- Expectations: how do we see evidence of a belief in effort-based intelligence show up in Practices, Behaviors, Structures and Staff Talk?
- Curriculum: what is the evidence that the Montgomery County Curriculum is being taught, managed, and adapted for students while maintaining high standards?
- Planning: what is the evidence that teacher planning is precise, flexible, aligned, and based on on-going analysis of student performance?

- Instruction: what is the evidence that there is a repertoire of instructional strategies matched to students appropriately?
- Evidence of Student Learning: what are the artifacts, samples, products and records of student learning in evidence besides grades?
- Professional Learning Community: what is the evidence that we are developing adult cultures of systematic examination of student work, non-defensive self-examination, reaching out to the knowledge base and shared responsibility for student learning? What is the evidence that we create time and structures so these qualities of courageous and supportive conversations can occur with frequency and depth?

With this framework, we have attempted to come back full circle to our opening proposition that the process is as much the point as the measurement of student results. We are asking tough questions about the things that matter, trying new strategies together, and focusing resources where they can do the most good…in each teachers' classroom and the development of an expert teacher for each child.

The assessment movement of the late 1990s made the point that data gathering about how students are doing, and feedback to them about their work must not be infrequent and episodic. So with us as professionals: assessment, self-assessment, and data gathering should be continuous. We are cultivating these habits of practice for the adults in Montgomery County as well as for the students.

Gathering data of the types above is not onerous, but it is a new feature of teacher evaluation in most districts. Therefore, we have offered training to all our evaluators in how to collect it as part of their daily rounds in the school as opposed to add-on chores to their already full days.

Training

Other training is required as well. Administrators and department chairs receive 72 hours of training in: (1) the skills of observing and analyzing teaching; (2) gathering data from multiple sources; (3) writing with a balance of claims, evidence, interpretations, and judgments; (4) differential conferencing; and (5) the importance of Professional Community to better teaching and thus better student results. The courses create a common language and concept system for dialog about teaching practice and are integrated with professional development offerings for teachers. It is important to note, however, that the purposes of the extensive professional development apparatus (15 full time in-house trainers who provide services to all teachers and administrators in the county) is not to prepare teachers for evaluation (i.e., to arm them to know what evaluators are expecting). The entire approach to the knowledge base is that it defines *repertoires of options* in important areas of performance, not singular "effective" behaviors that evaluators will come looking for with checklists. Capacity for insightful *analysis* of teaching, in all its complexity, is what these PD experiences develop, in both administrators and teachers alike. Beyond instructional strategies, beyond, classroom management, this knowledge base includes learning how to get low performing students to exert effective effort and to believe in themselves. It includes challenging our own beliefs about innate intelligence. And it includes the planning and design skills of good curriculum thinkers, which all teachers must also be. Lest one think 72 hours is an overdose of training, it is just the beginning of career long learning about expert teaching practice. But if we believe all children can learn, *really* believe that, then we must also provide every child with an expert teacher. So readers can see that we are attempting something very big here (i.e., to make real the promise to reach every child with the teaching they need). Including student results in teacher evaluation is but one component, albeit an essential one, of this larger mission.

So therefore, the purpose of the professional development offerings for teachers is to create professional communities of practice. In these communities, the knowledge base on teaching is used as a resource pool in which to dip when one needs something new to change teaching practice in light of student results.

Administrative Leadership That Puts a Premium on Developing Strong Professional Community, Especially:

- shared responsibility for student learning
- continual and systematic examination of student data
- respect for the complexity of teaching
- continuous and strong professional development
- norms of collegiality in the culture of the school

We have taken our lead from the thinking of Newmann and Wehlage (1995), Elmore (1996), Louis (2001), and many others who have consistently pointed to the linear correspondence between professional community and better student results. And why not; strong professional community directly leads to better teaching. And better teaching is the most powerful correlate of student achievement (Sanders 1996; Mendro 1998; Gross 1999).

Our training and supervision of administrators, therefore, focuses on how they facilitate a respectful collegial climate and strengthen these communities among faculty and staff. We conduct annual "school environment surveys" of faculty and staff that are combined with parent and student surveys to constitute a "quality" accountability measure for each school. Ultimately, we believe our evaluation of administrators must hold them accountable for good process as well as good product. Translation: show evidence you are fostering Professional Community in your building and teams; show evidence also that your student results are improving.

We know that we have a long way to go. We have yet to reach the majority of our teaching force with the staff development they desire on expanding repertoires of teaching skills (Studying Skillful Teaching I and II). We are only half-way through developing a evaluation system for administrators that mirrors what we have designed in the teachers' Professional Growth Cycle (i.e., the emphasis on building Professional Learning Community and improving teaching simultaneous to examination of student results). Yet we are confident we can keep these initiatives going because we are tackling this massive restructuring of teaching with joint ownership by the teachers association and the school department. The principals' association has a full-time release position for its leadership this year for the first time; we are hoping this will enable our building leaders to enter as full partners in planning this culture change as well.

Labor-Management Partnership

The subtext of this essay on students' results and teacher evaluation has been a culture change in our county, one that is far from complete. It is a culture change that shows up in allocation of resources, new structures, and new behaviors. It is a change that acknowledges and honors the complexity of teaching; it is a change that fosters courageous conversations, based on data, about how to improve instruction and, thus, student achievement; and it is a culture change of stepping up to the plate and claiming responsibility, joint responsibility, as teachers and administrators for student results. We would have made little progress on this journey, however, had we not had an unusual agreement from the outset, renewed each year and struggled with each year, between school board, teachers' union, and superintendent that we must share responsibility and continually support and push one another in the work. The design, implementation, and the evaluation of how we're doing with our new Professional Growth system has been a partnership from day one.

In 1996, a blue ribbon panel of citizens, school board members, administrators and teachers recommended a revision of the teacher evaluation system, which was based on a 1979 model. Research for Better Teaching, Inc. (RBT) of Acton, Massachusetts was hired in April of 1997 through a competitive process to design a new evaluation system for the county. Part of the attraction for RBT was the commitment of the county leaders, both union and administration, to be partners in accountability for student learning and to work actively to transform the workplace culture of the schools. From the outset, three union members from the teachers association and one from the principals' association were on the Steering Committee set up with high-level decision makers from the superintendent's cabinet to oversee the design process. Meeting monthly, the Steering Committee chartered the task as designing a Professional Growth Cycle that would include, but go far beyond, traditional teacher evaluation in its intent and structure. And so it has, including the operation of a full Peer Assistance and Review process (P.A.R.).

Management has taken risks and so has union leadership. As the Board and Superintendent entered a new level of partnership with the union, there was debate and divisiveness on the Board itself. Closeness with the teachers' union became an issue in school board elections. It became divisive within the PTA organization. But in spite of the continued nay-saying by a few, the public seems to prefer teamwork to conflict, and shared responsibility for quality to traditional adversarial roles. Sometimes slim BOE majorities, subjects, previously the exclusive province of management, became the subject of bi-lateral agreements. Weekly leadership meetings began to involve the unions. Important conversations routinely included the leadership of the three employee constituencies.

It has taken a clear articulation of the "new unionist" perspective by MCEA leadership, together with decent improvements in the bread-and-butter concerns of pay and benefits, to maintain the confidence of the rank-and-file. On-line debate has been continuous. But opposition has been isolated to a few individuals. The more significant result has been a new interest in the union from teachers who want to focus on being good teachers and would have been content to let others do the union activism. By gaining a foothold among teachers seeking an outlet for their professionalism and seeking more professional working conditions, the union has merged the concepts of professional organization and labor union.

Overall, the notion of "leadership" has been redefined. System leadership now includes the leadership of the teachers, administrators, and support staff unions. The notion of school leadership acknowledges that, "anyone, regardless of formal position, may exercise leadership". We talk of distributive leadership and facilitative leadership, and we are in the process of designing a "career lattice" that will allow teachers to exercise leadership with their peers while remaining in the classroom. All of this is a work in progress, but the important point is that we have crossed a threshold. Responsibility for the quality of teaching and student results will be a shared responsibility. In that context, it is natural to include student results as part of the dialogue with teachers about the quality of their work during their formal evaluation.

....

Becoming a data-based professional organization that focuses on student results has been the center of our culture change, along with shared responsibility for those results. In this essay, we have argued that this is the time to include student results in teacher evaluations. But "results" must be understood as far more than test scores. And teacher evaluation must be viewed as an element of a larger "system" focused on improving instruction. That "system" has structures, resources, and leadership to create a professional community with a high degree of ownership and commitment on the part of teachers, where courageous conversations and non-defensive self-examination of practice become the norm.

– Jon Saphier, Chairman of Teachers 21, and
President, Research for Better Teaching
– Mark Simon, President,
Montgomery County Education Association
– Jerry Weast, Superintendent,
Montgomery County Public Schools

Our thanks to Dr. Caroline Tripp of Research for Better Teaching
who made important contributions to the four
sample evaluations in this article.

Bibliography

DuFour, Richard and Robert Eaker. *Professional Learning Communities at Work: Best Practices for Enhancing Student Achievement.* Alexandria: ASCD, 1998.

Elmore, Richard and Deanna Burney. "Staff Development and Instructional Improvement, Community District 2, New York City." New York: National Commission on Teaching and America's Future, March 1996.

Gross, S. "Final Report, Mathematics Content/Connections Elementary Science in Montgomery County (Maryland): A Comprehensive Transformation of a System-wide Science Program." July 1999 (Published by Montgomery County Public Schools).

Kerchner, Charles Taylor, Julia E. Koppich and Joseph G. Weeres. *Taking Charge of Quality.* San Francisco: Jossey-Bass, 1998.

Kerchner, Charles Taylor, Julia E. Koppich and Joseph G. Weeres. *United Mind Workers.* San Francisco: Jossey-Bass, 1997.

Koppich, Julia E. "The Third Year of the MCPS Professional Growth System". Montgomery County Public Schools, 2004.

"Learning a Living: A Blueprint for High Performance". The Secretary's Commission on Achieving Necessary Skills (SCANS REPORT,) U.S. Department of Labor. Washington, D.C. April 1992.

Mendro, Robert and Karen Bebry. "School Evaluation: A Change in Perspective" Paper presented at the Annual Meeting of the American Educational Research Association (New Orleans, LA, April 24-28, 2000).

MCPS Professional Growth System Handbook. Montgomery County Public Schools, 2004.

Murnane, Richard and Frank Levy. *Teaching the New Basic Skills.* New York, N.Y.: The Free Press. 1996.

Newmann, Fred M. and Gary G. Wehlage, *Successful School Restructuring*. Madison, Wisconsin: Center on Organization and Restructuring of Schools, 1995.

Sanders, W.L. and J.C. Rivers, "Cumulative and Residual Effects of Teachers on Future Student Academic Achievement." Knoxville, TN: University of Tennessee Value-Added Research and Assessment Center, 1996.

Toole, J. C. and Karen Seashore. "The Role of Professional Learning Communities in International Education." Center for Applied Research and Educational Improvement, U. of Minn., 2001.

Other Available Publications

Research for Better Teaching Publications

- *The Skillful Teacher: Building Your Teaching Skills* (5th edition)
  by Jon Saphier and Robert Gower, 1997

- *How to Make Supervision and Evaluation Really Work:*
  Supervision and Evaluation in the Context of Strengthening School Culture
  by Jon Saphier, 1993

- *The Skillful Leader: Confronting Mediocre Teaching*
  by Alexander D. Platt, Caroline E. Tripp, Wayne R. Ogden, & Robert G. Fraser , 2000

- *How to Bring Vision to School Improvement: Through Core Outcomes, Commitments, and Beliefs*
  by Jon Saphier and John D'Auria, 1993

- *Activators:*
  Activity Structures to Engage Students' Thinking Before Instruction
  by Jon Saphier and Mary Ann Haley, 1993

- *Summarizers:*
  Activity Structures to Support Integration and Retention of New Learning
  by Jon Saphier and Mary Ann Haley, 1993

- *How to Make Decisions That Stay Made*
  by Jon Saphier, Tom Bigda-Peyton, and Geoff Pierson, 1993

Teachers[21] Publications

- *Beyond Mentoring: How to Attract, Support, and Retain New Teachers*
  by Jon Saphier, Susan Freedman, and Barbara Aschheim, 2001

- *Assessment in Practice: A View from the School*
  by Lynn F. Stuart, 2003

- *Mentoring Works: A Sourcebook for School Leaders*
  Edited by, Lynda Johnson, Susan Freedman, Barbara Aschheim, and Vicki Levy Krupp, Beginning Teacher Center of Teachers[21] and Simmons College, 2004